The Lucent Library of Historical Eras

Elizabethan England

# Life in Elizabethan London

## Other titles in The Lucent Library of Historical Eras, Elizabethan England, include:

Elizabeth I and Her Court
Great Elizabethan Playwrights
A History of the Elizabethan Theater
Primary Sources

The Lucent Library of Historical Eras

# Elizabethan England
# Life in Elizabethan London

Gail B. Stewart

LUCENT BOOKS®

THOMSON
™
GALE

San Diego • Detroit • New York • San Francisco • Cleveland • New Haven, Conn. • Waterville, Maine • London • Munich

THOMSON
——— ✶ ———™
GALE

© 2003 by Lucent Books. Lucent Books is an imprint of The Gale Group, Inc.,
a division of Thomson Learning, Inc.

Lucent Books® and Thomson Learning™ are trademarks used herein under license.

*For more information, contact*
Lucent Books
27500 Drake Rd.
Farmington Hills, MI 48331-3535
Or you can visit our Internet site at http://www.gale.com

**LIBRARY OF CONGRESS CATALOGING-IN-PUBLICATION DATA**

Stewart, Gail B., 1949–
    Life in Elizabethan London / by Gail B. Stewart
        p. cm. — (The Lucent library of historical eras: Elizabethan England)
    Summary: Looks at the daily life of those living in London, England, during the reign
of Elizabeth I, including a glimpse of what a first-time visitor might have noticed.
    Includes bibliographical references and index.
    ISBN 1-59018-100-X (hardback : alk. paper)
   1. London (England)—Social life and customs—16th century—Juvenile literature. 2.
London (England)—Social conditions—Juvenile literature. [1. London (England)—Social
life and customs—16th century. 2. London (England)—Social conditions.] I. Title.
II. Lucent library of historical eras: Elizabethan England.

  DA680 .S848 2003
  942.1'055—dc21

                2002011292

Printed in the United States of America

# Contents

# Foreword

Looking back from the vantage point of the present, history can be viewed as a myriad of intertwining roads paved by human events. Some paths stand out—broad highways whose mileposts, even from a distance of centuries, are clear. The events that propelled the rise to power of Germany's Third Reich, its role in World War II, and its eventual demise, for example, are well defined and documented.

Other roads are less distinct, their route sometimes hidden from view. Modern legislatures may have developed from old tribal councils, for example, but the links between them are indistinct in places, open to discussion and interpretation.

The architecture of civilization—law, religion, art, science, and government—as well as the more everyday aspects of our culture—what we eat, what we wear—all developed along the historical roads and byways. In that progression can be traced every facet of modern life.

A broad look back along these roads reveals that many paths—though of vastly different character—seem to converge at a few critical junctions. These intersections are those great historical eras that echo over the long, steady course of human history, extending beyond the past and into the present.

These epic periods of time are the focus of Lucent's Library of Historical Eras. They shine through the mists of history like beacons, illuminated by a burst of creativity that propels events forward—so bright that we, from thousands of years away, can clearly see the chain of events leading to the present.

Each Lucent Library of Historical Eras consists of a set of books that highlight various aspects of these major eras. For example, the Elizabethan England library features volumes on Queen Elizabeth I and her court, Elizabethan theater, the great playwrights, and everyday life in Elizabethan London.

The mini-library approach allows for the division of each era into its most significant and most interesting parts and the exploration of those parts in depth. Also, social and cultural trends as well as illustrative documents and eyewitness accounts can be prominently featured in individual volumes.

Lucent's Library of Historical Eras presents a wealth of information to young readers. The lively narrative, fully documented primary and secondary source quotations, maps, photographs, sidebars, and annotated bibliographies serve as launching points for class discussion and further research.

In studying the great historical eras, students also develop a better understanding of our own times. What we learn from the past and how we apply it in the present may shape the future and may determine whether our era will be a guiding light to those traveling future roads.

# Introduction
# Elizabeth's London

There is no doubt that London changed during the time of Queen Elizabeth I. Before Elizabeth came to the throne in 1558, London had been dismissed by most of Europe as a dull backwater—a city that could not compare in culture or excitement to the likes of Paris or Venice. Clearly unimpressed, one foreign visitor in 1545 had dubbed London "the arse of the world."[1]

But things changed drastically during Elizabeth's time. The Elizabethan era, as it was later called, was a time of growth for England—and nowhere was that growth more visible than in London. Between 1500 and 1600, the city's population ballooned from twelve thousand to two hundred thousand people. Not only was Elizabeth's London the largest city in England, but it also had become the most populated city in all of Europe.

The rapid rise in population, together with the booming economy of the Elizabethan era, transformed London from the dull, provincial place it had once been. Elizabeth's London became a bustling, complex city that encompassed the best and worst aspects of that age.

## Swans and an Architectural Marvel

Physically, London was very picturesque, especially as one approached the city. Its southern boundary was the Thames River, a shining blue ribbon of water on which all sorts of ships and barges moved. In his 1587 book *A Description of England*, William Harrison described a pleasant scene that could be witnessed on any day on the Thames: "In like manner I could entreet of the infinite number of swans daily to be seen upon this river, the two thousand wherries and small boats, whereby three thousand poor watermen are maintained through the carriage and recarriage of such persons as they pass or repass from time upon the same."[2]

The London Bridge, the only path across the Thames from the south, was nearly 350 yards long and was considered an architectural must-see in its day. The bridge, marveled one visitor, was unlike anything found in the rest of Europe, "having with the draw-bridge twenty arches made of squared stone, of height sixty foot and in breadth thirty foot, distant from one another twenty foot, compact and joined together with vaults and cellars. Upon both sides be houses builded, so that it seemeth rather a continual street than a bridge."[3]

## Vendors and Football Matches

Elizabethan London was a place of constant activity. Hundreds of merchants hawked everything from imported gloves for rich gentlemen to fine writing paper and colorful inks. Food vendors sold fresh milk, fish, or warm gingerbread to female shoppers.

In the fields and parks around the city, teens played tennis and held fencing matches, and crowds gathered to watch horse races and soccer (called football), although the violence of the latter was often shocking to the first-time spectator. "As concerning football playing," wrote one man in 1583, "I protest to you, it may rather be called a friendly kind of fight than a play or recreation, a bloody and murdering practice than a fellowly sport or pastime."[4]

*During the Elizabethan era, London was transformed from a provincial backwater into a populous and architecturally stunning city. This 1616 illustration captures the beauty and bustle of the city.*

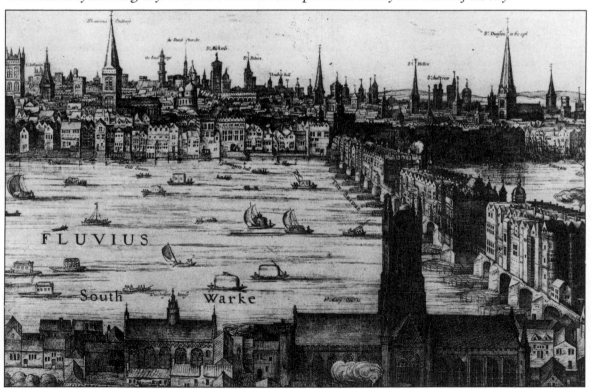

Dancers, jugglers, and bands of singers performed throughout the city. Playgoers could see a variety of dramatic entertainment—from bawdy musicals to the miracle plays with religious themes, to the contemporary plays of young William Shakespeare.

## Problems, Too

As beautiful and energetic as London was, however, it also had a dark side. The Londoner of Elizabeth's day saw not only the architectural marvel of London Bridge but also the grisly display of human heads on stakes above each gate to the bridge. The heads were displayed as a reminder of the bloody execution that awaited anyone found to be disloyal to the Crown.

In addition to the busy streets filled with vendors, pickpockets and cutpurses could strip shoppers of their money before they were aware of what was happening. And if pedestrians were not careful about where they stepped, they might slip on the slime and filth of the streets—deposited by those in homes above the shops who emptied their chamber pots out the windows each morning.

The constant noise of a city so large could be jarring, too. Some of it was pleasant, such as the calling and singing of the sellers and the "Westward Ho!" and "Eastward Ho!" of the boatmen drumming up business for their water taxis. But a great deal of London's noise was an unpleasant consequence of so many people crowded together. One wit-

*A portrait of Queen Elizabeth I. Elizabeth's London had all of the activity and problems common to the large cities of the age.*

ness wrote that in every London street "carts and coaches make such a thundering as if the world ran upon wheels . . . and hammers are beating in one place, tubs hooping in another, pots clinking in a third, water-tankards [water carts] running at tilt in a fourth."[5]

And although crime and noise were unpleasant aspects of life, nothing frightened Londoners as much as outbreaks of the plague, some of which were the worst that Europe would see. With no idea of how to cure or prevent the disease, residents were at the mercy of the plague. So many died, in fact, that to dispose of the body of a loved one who had fallen victim to the disease, one only had to hail one of the passing carts that traveled the streets. The cartman's cry of "Bring down your dead" became a noise as ordinary as those of the vendors selling their wares.

## Complex

As with any large modern city, Elizabethan London was made up of contrasting elements. There were wealthy people, including the queen and her court. Elizabeth dressed in gowns that were encrusted with tiny gems and held banquets in which live birds flew out of pastries for the amusement of her guests. Conversely, some Londoners lived on the streets, often lining up outside a wealthy man's home, hoping to catch table scraps discarded by the kitchen help.

Even though extreme wealth and abject poverty were visible in Elizabethan London, the majority of Londoners were somewhere in the middle. They were ordinary people, working long hours at jobs or in their homes, raising children, or going to school. They lived in homes in the narrow streets of the city or in the rural areas just outside of London. The way these people dealt with the complexities of their city—enduring its problems and reveling in its joys—gives an insight into Elizabethan London that is perhaps truer than any other.

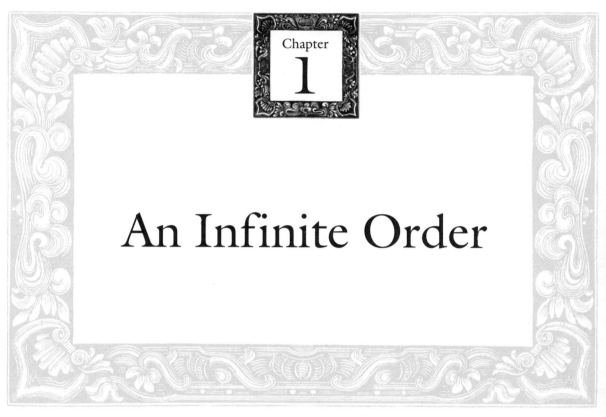

# An Infinite Order

When Elizabeth came to the throne in 1558, the English had a very definite view of how the world worked. Order and balance were extremely important; most people believed that throughout heaven and Earth there was an established hierarchy, or chain of importance. On the hierarchy, animals ranked below people while the angels ranked above. Each segment of the hierarchy had its own chain of importance, too. A lion, for instance, would rank higher than a rabbit, as a duke would outrank a beggar on the street. This ranking of social groups within society was a fact of life. Most people, whether rich or poor, accepted it without question. One was born to a particular level of English soci-

ety, and most of the time one had no choice but to remain there.

## From the Middle Ages

This worldview was not new to the Elizabethan era. In fact, the strict social system of the Middle Ages was based on this idea. During this period of history, which lasted roughly from the fifth century to the fifteenth, land—and people's relationship to it—was the key to social rank. All land was considered the monarch's property. He or she granted parcels of land, called landholdings, to certain elite individuals to be cared for and managed.

These elite landlords paid for the privilege of holding the land by offering military service whenever necessary, as one historian explains:

> When their lord [the monarch] called upon them, they were expected to come to him fully equipped as mounted knights with a following of soldiers. This was the gentlemanly form of service, and those who owed military service were considered to be of gentle birth, as was everyone in their families. Gentle status went hand in hand with political influence, social privilege, and cultural prestige.[6]

These gentlemen, in turn, had laborers to work the land. The laborers received a tiny portion of the crops they grew as well as a place to live. These laborers were often referred to as commoners. During the Middle Ages, a child born into a family of commoners would remain a commoner, just as a child born into a family of gentle birth would always have that status.

## The Monarchy and the Gentlemen

The social hierarchy in Elizabethan England was less rigid than that of the Middle Ages, but it still bore some similarities to the old system. The monarchy remained the highest rank. As in earlier times, kings and queens ruled by what was called divine right, which means that they were considered to hold power by the support of God.

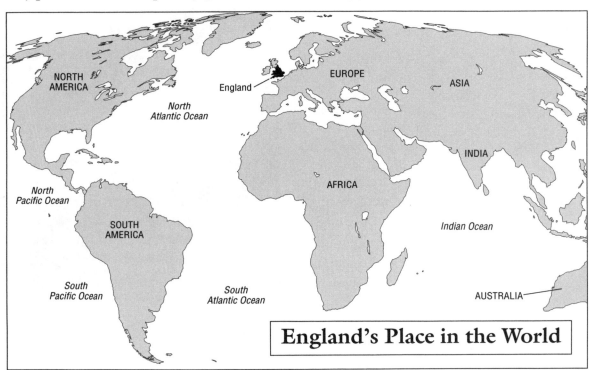

**England's Place in the World**

# The Advantages of Being a Nobleman

*Early during the seventeenth century, essayist Henry Peacham wrote about the rights and privileges of being a part of the noble class in London. This excerpt from* The Compleat Gentleman *is included in* Shakespeare's London, *edited by R.E. Pritchard.*

Noblemen or gentlemen ought to be preferred in fees, honours, offices and other dignities of command and government before the common people. . . . We ought to give credit to a noble or gentleman before any of the inferior sort. He must not be arrested or pleaded against upon cozenage [fraud]. We must attend him and come to his house, and not he to ours. His punishment ought to be more favourable and honourable upon his trial, and that to be by his peers of the same noble rank. He ought in all sittings, meetings, and salutations to have the upper hand and greatest respect. . . .

They ought to take their recreations of hunting, hawking, etc., freely, without control in all places. Their imprisonment ought to be in base manner, or so strict as others.

They may eat the best and daintiest meat that the place affordeth, wear at their pleasure gold, jewels, the best apparel and of what fashion they please, etc. . . . It is a spur in brave and good spirits to bear in mind those things which their ancestors have nobly achieved. It transferreth itself to posterity; and as for the most part, we see the children of noble personages to bear the lineaments [facial characteristics] and resemblance of their parents, so in like manner they possess their virtues and noble dispositions, which even in their tenderest years will bud forth and discover itself.

*Noblemen like Sir Philip Sidney enjoyed a life of privilege in London.*

Under the monarchy was the gentle class. In Elizabethan England, *gentleman* was usually defined as someone who did not need a job in order to live. As sixteenth-century historian and essayist Sir Thomas Smith explained, "Who can live idly and without manual labor and will bear the port, charge, and countenance [appearance] of a gentleman, he shall be called 'master,' for that is the title which men give to esquires and other gentlemen, and shall be taken for a gentleman."[7]

Gentlemen may have money because of landholdings, but there were several other acceptable ways to be thought of as a gentleman. Doing government service or being an officer in the queen's army or navy was considered gentlemanly. So was having a degree from a university or working in a professional field such law or medicine. The most profound difference between a gentleman of the Middle Ages and one of Elizabeth's era was that the rank was not always determined by one's birth. Though it was not easy, one could become part of the gentle class.

## A New Idea

For the first time there was actually a possibility—though not a likely one—for people to achieve a higher rank in society merely by accumulating money. This was important, for it signaled the beginning of a time when hard work and planning could help a member of a lower class—a merchant, perhaps—move into a higher one. As historian Elizabeth Burton explains, the age of Elizabeth was one in which membership in the gentle class was more and more an issue of money:

The great man was the rich man and he showed his greatness by the style and manner in which he lived. The Joneses weren't there to be lived up to. They were there to be ostentatiously surpassed. To be *nouveau riche* [newly rich, as opposed to rich by birth] was not to be despised, it was an admirable state— a goal which now could be achieved by almost any man nimble-witted, vigorous, enthusiastic, and lucky.[8]

In fact, some of the advisers of the Tudors (the royal dynasty that included Elizabeth) were themselves people of low birth who had worked hard to better themselves. Thomas Wolsey, who became the chancellor of England under Elizabeth's father, Henry VIII, was born into a poor family but became so wealthy, says one sixteenth-century writer, that he "travelled with twenty or more luggage mules and carts and carriages, yeomen [personal attendants] and servants in orange tawny coats embroidered with [his] initials."[9] Wolsey also entertained French ambassadors at his palace and was able to provide an astounding 280 beds for their sleeping accommodations.

## Prodigy Houses

Gentlemen did not all live in palaces as Wolsey did. But because one's home was an indicator of one's position, a gentleman did try to have as grand and showy a

*Thomas Wolsey (center, in bishop's robes) heads a procession in Westminster Abbey. Wolsey was born poor but accumulated enough wealth to rise to the class of gentlemen.*

place as possible. Thus, Elizabethan gentlemen built large estates with plenty of bay windows and open grounds.

Many new gentlemen built what were known as prodigy houses, country estates where they could entertain large numbers of guests at one time. Some even designed and upgraded their estates hoping that they might lure the queen herself to visit. Elizabeth made a yearly tour through some part of England, mostly to connect with the common people of her realm.

By stopping in for a visit on her tour at one of the prodigy houses, Elizabeth was guaranteed a few days of sumptious meals and entertainment without cost to her. In return, the host was guaranteed to be shown some favoritism—a title, some land, or even a lucrative business deal.

However, even though the host might have gained something, the cost of readying a house for the queen's visit was often immense, especially since she traveled with three hundred carts (each drawn by five or six horses) and a large staff of personal attendants. One man admitted in 1585 that he had spent the equivalent of thousands of dollars more than he ever intended on fashioning his home to suit the queen:

My house . . . was begun by me with a mean [thrifty] measure but increased by occasion of Her Majesty's often coming, whom to please I never would omit to strain myself to more charges than building it. And yet not without some special direction of Her

Majesty. Upon fault found with the small measure of her chamber (which was in good measure for me) I was forced to enlarge a room for a larger chamber.[10]

## Citizens

Below the class of gentlemen was the class known as citizens. These were most often tradesmen and craftsmen who had their own shops, and in modern times they would be known as the middle class. Citizens included grocers, booksellers, and jewelers. Although some made a great deal of money and were able to retire in a higher social class than the one in which they had begun their lives, most citizens in the time of Elizabeth remained in the middle class.

For every trade or craft there was a guild, sometimes called a livery company. The system of guilds, which was somewhat similar to modern labor unions, had developed during the Middle Ages. They were loose fellowships that helped citizens in the same occupation work out suitable prices for their work, standards of workmanship, as well as acceptable rules and practices for each trade. To set up trade in London or any other town in England, one had to be a member of a guild as well as pay a certain fee for the privilege of doing business.

A tradesmen or craftsmen and his family often lived in the same building as his shop, usually on the second floor. The second and third floors of the buildings were sometimes used by shop-workers, servants, or apprentices, who often ate their meals with the family. If a family had additional rooms, they might rent them to boarders, which was a common way for citizens to increase their income.

## Yeomen

The class of citizens did not exist in rural areas, even those close to the city. The equivalent of citizens among country people were yeomen (this is not to be confused with yeomen who were attendants to the wealthy). Yeomen were farmers; they might do some manual labor, but most of the time they were supervisors of lower-class workers.

The amount of land owned by a yeoman varied; a man with between fifty and one hundred acres was greatly admired by his peers. Men who owned fewer acres were often called husbandmen or cottagers. Their land was usually not enough to support them and their families, so they took on jobs as labors to supplement their income.

Some yeomen became very wealthy. As sixteenth-century writer William Harrison explains, the members of the yeoman class could be as financially successful as their city counterparts:

[The successful yeomen] commonly live wealthily, keep good houses, and travail [work hard] to get riches . . . insomuch that many of them are able and do buy the lands of unthrifty gentlemen, and often, setting their sons

# Entertaining the Queen at a Prodigy House

*It seems amazing that people spent so much time and money readying their homes for possible visits by Queen Elizabeth. Some were ridiculed by their neighbors for the expenses they incurred in making lavish improvements, especially when the queen was critical of those improvements. One such instance is described by Elizabeth Burton in* The Pageant of Elizabethan England.

The Queen had given [Sir Thomas Gresham] Osterley Park, once owned by an Abbess of Syon. Here Gresham built a magnificent house and when it was completed in 1577 the Queen came to see what it was like. The house apparently met with her approval but the courtyard, she thought, was far too big and would be greatly improved if divided by a wall. Having said this, she supped [ate] and went off to bed. What does Sir Thomas do? "In the night time, sends for workmen to London who so speedily and silently applied their business" that next morning the court was double which the night before was single.

Thus, says the commentator, "money commands all things." . . . But the Queen was pleased with the house and the divided courtyard and stayed several days. Gresham entertained her sumptuously [lavishly]. There were rides in the new park which had been made by enclosing Hounslow Heath [a nearby park], there was the heronry [nesting area for herons] to be admired and the ornamental ponds. There was a great banquet and a play was performed before her.

But one unfortunate incident happened—some of the local inhabitants who resented the enclosure of Hounslow Heath set fire to Gresham's new park palings [fencing]. This so annoyed the Queen that she clapped four men into prison for it. She might object to a feature [of the house], herself, but no one else could—and get away with it.

*Sir Thomas Gresham (pictured) made extensive improvements to his country estate to please Queen Elizabeth.*

to the schools, to the universities, and to the Inns of Court [law careers], or otherwise leaving them sufficient lands whereupon they may live without labor, do make them by those means to become gentlemen.[11]

## The Lower End of Society

Servants and laborers ranked below the citizens and yeomen. In the city these were the unskilled workers who were hired to carry water into homes, sweep and clean sidewalks and streets, and do other jobs. In the country, they were the milk-

maids, the shepherds, and the harvesters on farms. These people made up the majority of the population—about one-third of it—during the sixteenth century. Those who found employment as a servant in a citizen's home (or the home of someone even higher on the social scale) were lucky. They usually had job security. A cook or housekeeper, for instance, knew that if she did her job well she would not only receive steady wages, but she also would have a small room to live in within the family's home. Servants in gentlemen's or citizen's homes were also luckier than

*Servants create a meal in an Elizabethan kitchen. The unskilled workers of the lower classes occupied the menial positions of Elizabethan England.*

others in that they were usually outfitted very well. A man's servants tended to reflect the man's household, and a master dressing a stable boy or a valet in rags would be as socially embarrassing as dressing his own children that way.

Laborers, on the other hand, were less likely to have steady work. Many of the jobs available to them were seasonal, especially those on farms. As a result, they often were forced to move around in search of employment. It was not unusual for a laborer to be unemployed and homeless for part of the year. At the bottom of the social ladder, the laborers had no representation either in the government or in guilds. They had, reports Harrison, "neither voice nor authority in the commonwealth, but are to be ruled and not to rule others."[12]

## Under Society's Ladder

In the same class as the unemployed laborer were the poor and the homeless—those who survived by begging. These people were not even considered to have a place on the social ladder but were rather considered to be underneath it. More than 10 percent of the population in rural areas and 20 percent in London and other towns fell into this category. Besides the unemployed laborers, some were disabled. Many of these were itinerant, begging their way from house to house across the country.

During the time of Elizabeth, the wandering beggars and vagabonds had become a problem. Both cities and rural areas swarmed with a variety of wanderers, all hoping for charity from the general population. The most pitiful were the insane, who were often completely incapable of taking care of themselves and often lost—or were stripped of—any money that they might have been given by a sympathetic passerby.

Some of these people were former inmates of London's Bethlehem Hospital, where treatment of the insane meant beating or whipping them and keeping them in leg irons. (*Bethlehem* was pronounced "Bedlam," and because of the screaming and shouting coming from the hospital, that word has come to mean any situation of chaos or loud confusion.) Occasionally, when the hospital became overcrowded, the staff would give some of their patients official licenses to beg on London's streets.

Although these "bedlam beggars," as they were called, were authentic, a number of sane beggars chose to imitate them, creating what seemed like a competition to see who could look the most deranged—and thereby evoke the pity of the population. These bogus beggars were, remarked one historian, "an almost unbelievably numberous crew of rascals, who swarmed over the whole countryside practising the gentle art of living . . . at the expense of the respectable members of the community."[13]

## Clapperdudgeons and Abraham Men

One of the most frightening of this class of phony bedlam beggars were the clapperdudgeons. A clapperdudgeon actually

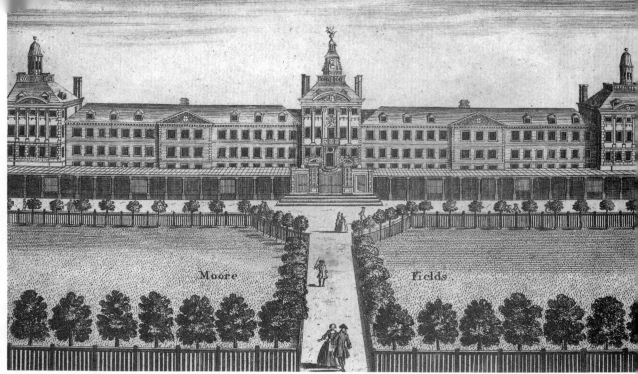

*The façade of London's Bethlehem Hospital. Many of Elizabethan London's beggars were former inmates of this mental asylum, which became known as "Bedlam."*

mutilated his own body, deliberately creating oozing sores on his arms and legs to make himself look as pathetic as possible.

To make these sores, the clapperdudgeon put arsenic on an ankle or an arm and waited until the skin became irritated. After that, he would tie foul or bloody rags around the skin so that the sores would become infected and, writes William Harrison, "move the hearts of goers-by such places where they lie, to yearn at their misery, and thereupon bestow large alms [donations] upon them."[14]

Another of these scam artists was known as an Abraham man. An Abraham made himself look as confused and odd as he could, both in his dress and the things he carried as he ambled down the street. As one sixteenth-century writer described him, "He walketh bare armed and bare legged, and carrieth a pack of wool or a stick with bacon on it or such like toy."[15] Another complains that the Abraham men so unnerve city residents that Londoners will give the odd-acting beggars anything just so they will leave. "When [the Abraham men] come to any door a-begging," he insists, "nothing is denied them."[16]

## "The Paradise of Married Women"

Although one's status in Elizabethan England was determined by one's social class, it was also determined by one's gender. Women had no social standing at all, aside from that of their husbands or, if they were unmarried, from that of their fathers. They did not inherit money or land; those things were passed down to

21

*A portrait of an Elizabethan woman. Women of the age had no social standing in their own right.*

explained one sixteenth-century essayist, "nature hath made to keep home . . . and not to meddle with matters abroad, nor to bear office in a city or commonwealth no more than children or infants."[17]

Even though such a view was quite typical throughout Europe during that time, some visitors to England during the Elizabethan era found that, although Englishwomen had no legal rights, they were often treated well. One Dutch observer wrote that, in some ways, Englishwomen had more freedom than women in other countries:

> They are not kept so strictly as they are in Spain or elsewhere. Nor are they shut up. . . . They go to market to buy what they like best to eat. They are well-dressed, fond of taking it easy, and . . . sit before their doors, decked out in fine clothes, in order to see and be seen by the passers-by. . . . This is why England is called "The Paradise of Married Women."[18]

sons rather than daughters. If for some reason a father did leave money to a daughter, it was put into a dowry and given to the daughter's husband when she married.

In every family, the Elizabethans believed, there were those who made the rules and those who must obey the rules. There was little doubt that women belonged in the latter category. "Women,"

Though some of this might have been true for the upper classes, the lives of the majority of women consisted of far more than fine clothes and marketing. For these women, managing a home and family bore little resemblance to a paradise.

# Marriage and Family

Marriage was a landmark for Elizabethans, for it was then that they acquired their real status in the society. Although women had no official status of their own, they were extremely important in running the household and in raising children, especially in the middle and lower classes. For a man, marriage meant he was no longer the dependent son of his parents. As a married man, he was an independent head of his household.

## Some Arranged, Some Not

The age at which young people could marry without their parents' consent was very young: fourteen for boys and twelve for girls. Even so, it was only the highest rungs of the upper class, for which marriages were arranged for political or economic reasons, that such young marriages took place.

Most Elizabethans married much later. The average age for a woman of the lower or middle classes to marry was about twenty-two; for a man, the average was about twenty-five. And because of the high death rate from diseases in those days, widows or widowers in their thirties were common. A healthy person who lived to be seventy might be married several times during his or her life.

Although most marriages among the common people were not arranged by parents, the idea of marrying for love was not common. For a great many people,

## "Duties of a Husband"

*Women were viewed by Elizabethan society as weak and incapable of making decisions. In the following excerpt from an essay by an Elizabethan man, the author explains the inherent weaknesses of women and why it was the husband's solemn duty to take care of his wife. The excerpt is contained in Allardyce Nicoll's book* The Elizabethans.

[A husband must] give honor to his wife as the weaker vessel, for she is partaker of the grace of life. . . . He must patiently brook the hastiness of his wife, for there is nothing in the world more spiteful than a woman if she be hardly dealt withal, or egged to indignation. . . . The husband must not injure his wife by word or deed, for a woman is a feeble creature and not endued with such a noble courage as the man; she is sooner pricked to the heart, or moved to passions, than man. . . . The husband must suffer his wife to be merrily disposed before him, otherwise (a woman's nature is such) she will by stealth find out some secret place or other to tattle in and disport herself.

But what shall the woman do? Shall she do what seemeth good in her own eyes? No, for St. Peter speaketh unto wives in this wise: "Let wives be subject to their husbands"—which is as much to say as they must not contradict them in any point, but rather to please them by all means. . . . She must esteem the manners of her husband to be the legal rules of her life.

marrying someone was a way to become independent of the parents' home—to start a life of one's own. Most people hoped that once a couple married and began setting up a home together, love and affection would follow.

## "I Like My Choice, I Will Not Change"

The marriage process had several steps. First, a betrothal, or engagement ceremony, had to take place before witnesses. The two people joined hands and pledged that they would marry. This agreement was considered a legal contract. Even though no marriage ceremony had taken place, someone who later changed his or her mind about the betrothal could be taken to a church-run court and punished, often in the form of a public apology.

Just as in modern times, a man would usually give a betrothal gift to the woman. Sometimes it was a ring, but just as often it might be a bracelet or a pair of gloves. If a ring was given—especially in the gentle class—the man might have the inside engraved with a poem or message. One popular message (which must have been very tiny, given the length of it) read:

Love is fix'd; I will not range
I like my choice, I will not change,
Wit, health, and beauty, all do dwell
But constant Love doth far excel.[19]

Once a couple was betrothed, they exchanged a number of little gifts. Usually those gifts were personal ones, such as handkerchiefs, flowers, or even a lock of hair.

## Banns and a Procession

After the betrothal, the couple had to wait for the minister to announce the marriage in church on three successive Sundays. Announcing the marriage this way was called crying the banns (*banns* was a very old word that meant "proclamation"). If the man and woman lived in different parishes, the banns had to be read in both. The purpose of the banns was to give anyone with a reason why the couple should not marry an opportunity to come forward. The couple may be too closely related, for example, or one of them might already be betrothed (or even married) to someone else.

Once the banns had been read three times, the wedding was allowed to take place. Friends and relatives were invited, and preparations were made. The bride wore her best dress, and although white was allowed, it was not a common color for a gown. Many brides chose gowns in a brownish pink shade, called russet. Before

the wedding, the bridesmaids gathered to sew little ribbons of various colors on the dress, and after the ceremony each of the bachelors in attendance ran to the bride to pull off one of the ribbons. This was considered a sign that the bachelors who got a ribbon would soon marry—similar to the modern-day custom of a bride throwing her bouquet. Each of the lucky bachelors displayed his ribbon on his hat for several days after the wedding.

During the Elizabethan era, weddings were always performed in churches by ministers. The wedding party, made up of close friends and family, gathered at a meeting place—usually the bride's home—and then proceeded to the church in a group. The procession was usually loud, with singing, laughter, and often bawdy jokes.

## "The Scumm of Our Parish" and "a Dumbe Person"

Because churches in those days did not have seats or pews, everyone stood during the ceremony. Church doors were always open, too, and that meant anyone could attend the ceremony. Strict attention was paid to the social ladder, though, and the lower classes stood in the back of the church, by the doors.

The ceremony itself was short, and after it concluded, the event was made official as the parish clerk recorded the details. Some of these entries in parish chronicles have survived for centuries and provide an interesting look at the attitudes of the time. For instance, the official church records of one London church contain a record of two beggars who were married at the church. The marriage was recognized by the church, although the clerk dismissed the event by referring to the couple as "both of the Scumm of our parish."[20]

In another entry, the clerk of the church described a most unusual wedding of a man named Thomas Speller:

*A contemporary portrait of a young married couple. Most marriages in Elizabethan England were arranged for reasons of convenience.*

I have sett downe the order of this Mariage at long, because wee never had the like. [Speller was] a dumbe person by trade a Smith [blacksmith], of Hatfield Broadoake, in the Countie of Essex, and Sara Earle, daughter to John Earle . . . were married. . . . And the said Thomas Speller the Dumbe partie, his willingness to have the said Mariage rites solemnized [made official], appeared, by bringing the Booke of Common Prayer (and his license) in one hand, and his Bride in the other unto the Minister of our Parish. . . . and made the best signes he could, to show that he was willing to be maried.[21]

The final part of the day was the wedding feast. In the country, the guests pitched in and helped with the food and drink. William Harrison, a writer of the day, describes one such feast as offering so many choices that "it is incredible to tell what meat is consumed and spent, each one bringing such a dish or so many with him."[22] Sometimes to help defray the costs of the event, the bride sold cups of ale to whatever guests were willing to pay. All proceeds, of course, would help the couple begin their new life together.

## Babies

Most couples wanted children, if not for sentimental reasons, then for economic ones. Even though it certainly cost more to expand the household, children could help out a great deal as they got older.

# "So Ended This Miserable Life"

*The death of a child was a common occurrence during Elizabethan times. In this brief paragraph, quoted in R.E. Pritchard's book* Shakespeare's England, *Nehemiah Wallington, a young father, describes how quickly his young son became sick and died.*

On the twenty-fifth day of March . . . it pleased the Lord to afflict my son John so that he was very sick and ate nothing for one whole week, but only took some cold beer. The night before he died, he lay crying all that night, "Mame [Mommy], O John's hand! O John's foot!" for he was struck cold all one side of his body; and about three o'clock in the morning Mistress Trotter that watch[ed] with him wakened my wife and I and told us he was a-departing now. And my wife started up and looked upon him; he then being aware of his mother, he said, "Mame, John fall down, opaday [Oh oh!]. Mame, John fall down, opaday." And the next day he had two or three fits, that we thought he would have died at that time, and at eleven o'clock at night he said unto the maid, "Jane, some beer," and she gave him some beer. Then he said, "Opaday!" These are the last words that my sweet son John spake; and so ended this miserable life on Tuesday the fifth day of April.

Sons helped the father in the family trade, and daughters helped their mothers cook, clean, and look after the younger children.

Having children was not taken for granted, however. Although there was a high birth rate (the average woman was pregnant six times during her life), there was also a high death rate. Disease was commonplace in Elizabethan London, and about one-fourth of all children died before their tenth birthday. Mothers, too, were at risk; 1 percent in country areas died in childbirth, and because of the unsanitary conditions in the city, almost 3 percent died in London.

The high death rate was one important reason babies were baptized, or christened, quickly (only a week or two after birth). The parents of the child asked three trusted adults to come to the church to stand as godparents—two of the same sex as the baby, and one of the opposite sex. After the minister performed the ceremony, parents held a christening feast for family and friends. Well-wishers customarily brought presents for the newborn. One of the most popular gifts during the sixteenth century was an apostle spoon, the end of which had the likeness of one of the twelve apostles. A common present in wealthy families was a piece of coral mounted on a silver handle, often with tiny bells attached. Besides being a beautiful remembrance of the occasion, the gift was practical, for coral was often used to soothe teething or fretful babies.

Babies were also officially named on their christening day; until that time, it was not unusual for a child to be simply referred to as "the infant" or "Baby." Many of the most common names for boys were those of former kings: William, Humphrey, Richard, Henry, Arthur, and Hugh. The most common names for girls were often biblical: Anne, Margaret, Mary, and Catherine.

## Advice for New Parents

Parents in Elizabethan times usually raised their children in a much different manner than parents of today, and the differences started almost immediately after birth. Elizabethans considered it crucial for babies to be wrapped securely in long bands of linen so that they could not move their arms and legs freely. A baby with freedom of movement while lying in her crib was believed to be in danger of growing improperly, with curved or deformed limbs. "If [the infant] be bound and swaddled," writes one expert of the time, "the members [limbs] lying right and straight, then shall it grow straight and upright; if it be crookedly handled, it will grow likewise."[23]

Once children were old enough to walk and talk, there was a great deal expected of them. They were expected to be well behaved, especially in dealing with parents and other adults. Parents taught their children the proper forms of address, such as "sir" and "madam" for a person of a higher rank. Children were expected to stand when approached by an adult and to curtsy, or bend one knee, when being introduced to someone new.

Many historians have noted that Elizabethan-era children were treated more like small adults than children. "Childhood," writes one authority, "like the diseases incident to it, was a thing to be got over as quickly as possible."[24] In the upper classes, many children even dressed in the same style of clothing as their parents and modeled their parents' behavior.

Misbehavior among children was cause for immediate discipline. To the Elizabethan parent, discipline was usually physical—a spanking or a cuff on the back of the head were common punishments. Most parents believed the words of William Vaughan, a well-known author of the time, who urged them to "chastise the child and imprint discipline in his heart while he is young . . . and thou shalt bow him to what instruction thou wilt."[25]

## Off to School

When children reached the age of five, they sometimes began their education, although school was a voluntary activity in Elizabethan times. There was no nationwide system of schools, nor did people yet believe that an educated public made a strong country. Some children, especially those in lower-class working families, never attended school; their parents believed they would never really need an education to do the kinds of jobs for which they were destined. But if a parent thought the child could perhaps grow to own his own business (and increase his social standing), then an education was a must.

When Elizabeth came to the throne, the English population was not a well-educated one. A survey taken in 1580 found that only 16 percent of women in London could even sign their names. Only about 20 percent of men and 5 percent of women could read and write. As the standard of living improved and many saw that education could help them achieve greater success, the numbers of educated people increased. By the end of Elizabeth's reign, 30 percent of men and 10 percent of women were literate.

## Petty Schools

Nobles and others of the gentle class usually were taught by private tutors. However,

*A portrait of a wealthy Elizabethan family. Children of the upper strata of Elizabethan society modeled their dress and behavior on that of their parents.*

# Instructions to Children and Servants

*In his book* The Tudor Age, *A.F. Scott includes an excerpt from a book of manners for children and servants in a household, written by Hugh Rhodes in 1577. As with many instructive books of the day for both children and adults, it is written in rhyme.*

When that thou comest to the Church, thy prayers for to say,
See thou sleepe not, nor yet talke not, devoutly looke thou pray,
Ne cast thine eyes to ne fro, as thinges thou wouldst still see;
So shall wise men judge thee a foole, and wanton for to be.
When thou are in the Temple, see thou do they Churchly works,
Heare thou God's word with diligence, crave pardon for they faults.

Look that your knife be sharp and kene to cut your meate withall;
So the more cleanlyer, be sure, cut your meate you shall.
Or thou put much bread in thy pottage, looke thou doe it assay [easy];
Fill not thy spoone to full, lest thou lose somewhat by the way.

Fill not they mouth to full leaste thou perhaps of force must speak;
Nor blow not out thy crums when thou doest eate.
Foul not the place with spitting whereas thou doest sit,
Least it abhore some that sit by; let reason rule thy wit.
If thou must spit, or blow thy nose, keepe thou it out of sight,
Let it not lie upon the ground, but tread thou it out right.

most English children attended the petty school. It was there that they learned the basics of reading, writing, and adding and subtracting, which was known then as ciphering.

Many petty schools were run under the auspices of a church nearby; in 266 parishes during the time of Elizabeth, 113 of them had a petty school. A schoolmaster would seek a license from the church hierarchy, which gave him permission to use the church facilities for classes. Similar schools were run by women in their homes and were known as dame schools.

Most petty-school students were boys, although it was common for there to be a few girls in a class. The students were between the ages of five and seven. They came to school with a goose quill, some ink, and a little knife that they used to sharpen the feather into a penpoint. (This type of knife is still referred to as a penknife.)

The school provided what was known as a hornbook—a wooden paddle onto which a page of instruction was attached. The paper was protected by a thin, translucent sheet of horn, giving the device its name. The hornbook had the alphabet printed on it as well as the Lord's Prayer and assorted Bible verses. Children held the hornbook and recited from it, both individually and as a group.

## "Utterly Ignorant"

Some people of the time were disdainful of the teachers of these schools. They insisted that the teachers were not qualified and were only slightly more educated than the young children they were instructing. One educator wrote that English children "almost everywhere are first taught either in private by men or women altogether rude, and utterly ignorant of the due composing and just spelling of words."[26]

No matter how educated the teachers were, however, they were strict disciplinarians. Every dame school and petty school had a birch rod in the corner, and the teachers did not usually hesitate to use it on the backs of students who caused trouble in the class or who were slow to learn.

## Options

For many children in the middle or lower classes, two years of petty school was enough; they had a basic idea of the rules of

*Elizabethans used the hornbook, a one-page primer, to teach the basics of reading.*

reading and arithmetic. Girls almost always stopped going to school after age seven. They were expected to stay home with their mothers and learn to sew, cook, and manage a home so that they would be good wives and mothers someday. Occasionally a girl might continue her formal education, but almost never past the age of nine.

Boys, too, often stopped school after two years of petty school. If a boy had no plans to work as a merchant, or any other job that required him to read or do arithmetic, his two-year stint was more than enough education. If he was a country boy, he dropped out to help his father on the farm. Even at age six or seven, boys could be helpful in stacking grain, clearing stones from fields, and so on.

City boys whose education stopped after petty school stayed home and helped with chores—carrying water, tending fires, and helping watch younger brothers and sisters. As they grew, their responsibilities increased; by age thirteen or fourteen, they were almost always working full time as an apprentice learning a trade.

## The Twelve-Hour School Day

Some boys did continue their education, however. For boys who enjoyed learning—or, more important, for those whose parents were eager for their sons to better their social position—the next step was the grammar school. Grammar schools were so called because the focus was on the grammar of Latin, then considered to be the universal language of the learned. Latin was the language of the church, of medicine and science, and of philosophy. And because it was so widely spoken by scholars, a boy who knew Latin during Elizabethan times could travel to any country in Europe and be understood.

Besides learning the complex grammar of Latin, students in grammar schools studied literature by great Roman writers, such as Virgil, Horace, and Livy.

The boys also studied Greek, mathematics, and ancient history.

The school day was extremely long; students were to be sitting at their form, or bench, by 6:00 each morning. The students worked until about 9:00 and then broke for fifteen minutes for breakfast. There was another break between 11:00 and noon for lunch, and then the boys worked until 5:30 or 6:00, when classes were finally over. If the grammar school was a day school, the students went home to dinner; if it was a boarding school, the boys ate and went back to the dormitory, where they read or studied until bedtime.

The threat of discipline, especially physical punishment, was even stronger in grammar school than it had been in petty school. One student claimed that the schoolmasters found many reasons to beat the boys: "I knew one [teacher] who in winter would ordinarily, in a cold morning, whip his boys over for no other purpose than to get himself a heat; another beat them for swearing, and all the while swears himself, with horrible oaths, he would forgive any fault saving that."[27]

At age fourteen, boys left grammar school. Some, especially those with an interest in law or politics, continued on to one of the two English universities: Cambridge or Oxford. Others began work, learning a career that would enable them to buy a house or open a shop and earn enough money to think about starting a family of their own.

# A London Home

Whereas wealthy citizens bought large homes with gardens and fountains around them, the middle and lower classes often had homes above shops on narrow city streets. These houses had no numbered addresses, but colorful signs hanging above the doors of the shops made it easy for people to locate a particular house.

The houses were very close together, and tradesmen and merchants almost always lived behind or above their shops. The houses were small, and privacy was a rarity. Parents shared their bedrooms and often their beds with younger children; servants and apprentices usually lived in the home, too.

## Dirt, Crumbs, and Filth

Floors of London homes were either wood or stone. To make the floors feel warmer and softer, people spread a thick coat of rushes or straw on the floors. But although this was easier on the feet, the rush floors tended to have an unpleasant smell. Many wives tried to combat the problem by spreading a mixture of herbs and wildflowers among the rushes; lavender, pennyroyal, and basil were very popular. The rushes attracted bugs, too—especially fleas—and wives often spread strong-smelling wormwood plants on top of the rushes to kill the pests. One popular rhyme of the day explains:

While wormwood hath seed,
    get a bundle or twain,
To save against March, to make flea
    to refrain,
Where chamber is swept and that
    wormwood is strown,
No flea for his life dare abide to be
    known.[28]

Even so, some visitors to English homes often complained about the smell and the texture of the flooring, especially because the rushes acted as a magnet, collecting dirt, crumbs, and other filth. One man described the floor of a large country house as containing the stink of dogs and the droppings of birds. Dr. Andrew Boorde, who published a manual of healthy tips for homemakers during the mid-1500s, urged wives to solve the problem by sweeping out the floor covering regularly rather than simply adding another layer. He warned wives not to sweep until their husbands had gone out, however, "for the dust doth putrify the air, making it dense."[29]

## Light and Heat

Glass windows became very popular during Elizabethan times, and wealthy citizens spent a great deal of money building homes with many windows. Londoners even had a jingle about one large estate: "Hardwick Hall, more glass than wall."[30] Historians speculate that after so many years of the dark, almost windowless castles of medieval times, the English were happy to build homes with something other than defense in mind.

Only the upper class could afford to install so many windows, however. Most people had only one or two, and their homes were very dark, even during the day. People depended on candles and oil lamps for artificial light.

All houses—no matter how wealthy their owners—lacked central heating systems. People burned wood or coal in stoves or fireplaces, and more homes were being built with chimneys to carry the smoke and sparks away—a convenience that did not please everyone. William Harrison complained that the smoke-filled rooms of the past had not only strengthened the home's structure, but the thick smoke also made its inhabitants healthier:

Now we have many chimneys, and yet our tenderlings [open fireplaces]; and our heads did never ache. For as the smoke in those days was supposed to be a sufficient hardening for the timbers of the house, so it was reputed to be a far better medicine to keep the goodman and his family from the quack [doctor].[31]

## Tapestries and Cloths

The queen's residences and some of the huge prodigy houses contained many rooms, including indoor courtyards, large dining halls, gentlemen's parlors, libraries, bedroom suites, and so on. However, inside most homes there were only a few small rooms that could be used as bedrooms, and there was a hall, which was a sort of sitting room and eating area com-

*Hardwick Hall in Chesterfield is renowned for its large number of glass windows. Windows were a luxury item that only wealthy Elizabethans could afford.*

bined. Some homes had a kitchen inside, although the middle and upper classes—as well as country dwellers—had kitchens separate from the rest of the house. In all homes, one room simply led to another; passageways or hallways were rare, as were doors between rooms.

The ceilings and walls of most homes were plaster, but in the houses of the wealthy they were paneled with intricately carved oak. No one had paintings on their walls; landscapes and portraits did not become common until the mid-1700s. Instead, people hung tapestries on their walls—the more colorful, the better. Some had elephants, tigers, and other fantastic beasts embroidered on them; others depicted historical events, fables, and characters from Greek mythology, such as the goddess of the hunt and her dogs.

The commoners, however, generally could not afford tapestries. Instead, they often hung colorful cloths or curtains. Such hangings not only gave color to the rooms, but they also made the rooms a bit warmer by insulating the walls.

## Less Is More

The furniture in Elizabethan homes was usually made of a hardwood such as oak, walnut, or elm. Although these woods today are expensive materials for building, in sixteenth-century England they were both plentiful and cheap. The rooms would have looked quite empty by modern standards, for even wealthy people tended to buy fewer possessions. They preferred to spend more money buying a few items of quality, generally well-made, ornately carved furniture.

*An Elizabethan woman seated in an ornate chair performs a duet with her partner. Unlike this one, many chairs were armless to accommodate the ballooning hoopskirts in fashion at the time.*

The hall, which was the largest room in most homes, always had a long, narrow table where the family and guests ate their meals. Interestingly, there was only one real chair (with a back and arms) at the table, and that was reserved for the master of the house. The wife, children, and any guests sat on backless stools or benches.

Chairs in other parts of the house were likely to have backs but no arms. They were called farthingales, named after popular hoopskirts of the time. Women wearing the skirts could not fit into armed chairs, so the farthingale chair was created to solve that problem. Farthingales and other chairs were not upholstered. Instead, people put thin cushions or rugs on the chairs to make sitting more comfortable.

The hall also had wooden cupboards for storing pots, pans, knives, and linen. Some cupboards had glass doors, for people were proud to show off serving dishes and silver they acquired. As William Harrison notes, the beautiful displays were found in many houses, not only in those belonging to the wealthy:

In the houses of knights, gentlemen, [and] merchantmen. . . . it is not [uncommon] to behold generally their great provision of . . . pewter, brass, fine linen, and thereto costly cupboards of plate, worth five or six hundred, or a thousand pounds. Even the inferior artificers and many farmers have, for the most part, learned also to garnish their cupboards with plate.[32]

## From Pallets to Multimattresses

Elizabethan bedrooms had no closets; most people had only two or three changes of clothes, and these were kept in low wooden chests. As with chairs in the rest of the house, these chests were often covered with thick cloths or blankets so they could also be used as benches.

The bed, more than any other piece of furniture, changed dramatically during the sixteenth century—especially the beds of the middle class. Before the Elizabethan era, most people slept on thin straw mattresses. Harrison recalled that "our fathers, yea and we ourselves also, have lain full oft upon straw pallets, on rough mats covered only with a sheet."[33] And whereas the poorest citizens still slept on beds such as those, most Elizabethans had a far more comfortable

*A gentleman has his beard trimmed in the comfort of his bedroom. The curtains surrounding the bed are designed to keep out the night air, regarded by the Elizabethans as unhealthy.*

night's sleep than mats or pallets could provide.

Their beds were large, with a heavy frame of wood. Bed springs had not been invented, so rope, leather, or durable cloth was strung on the frame to support first a mattress stuffed with either straw or wool. On top of this was a feather mattress (sometimes two), which would be covered in linens. Pillows, which a generation before had been dismissed as useful only to women in childbirth, were now used by many people, although one observer noted that many farmers continued to use "a good round log under their heads instead of a . . . pillow."[34]

Beds usually had curtains hung around them on every side. People believed night air to be unhealthy. In addition, bedrooms were cold places at night after fires were put out, and bed curtains kept drafts away. Besides using curtains to warm up the bed on a winter evening, one might use a warming pan, a covered device that could be filled with hot coals and left under the covers to warm the cold linens.

Finally, many large beds had trundles, or low, thin beds, underneath them. These trundles could be pulled out and used by children or even by a servant or an attendant. They were handy since they could be pushed back under the large bed during the day.

## No Running Water

Perhaps the most inconvenient aspect of life in Elizabethan times was the lack of running water. People who lived on farms near London drew the water they needed from wells or streams, but getting water in London was a more involved task. City water came—either directly or indirectly—from the rivers and streams around London, including the Thames. Large pipes or conduits, made either of lead or of hollowed-out logs, carried water to various cisterns, or holding tanks, around the city and were usually located on busy streets.

The wealthiest homes had their own conduits that brought water to large fountains on their estates. The middle classes had to carry water by hand from the conduits or cisterns to their homes. To do this job, they hired water carriers, who were known as cobs. Observed one visitor to London in 1592, "The poor water-bearers carry it on their shoulders to the different houses and sell it in a peculiar kind of wooden vessels, broad at the bottom, but very narrow at the top, and bound with iron hoops."[35] The poorest citizens, who had neither servants nor money to hire cobs, simply dipped their bucket into the cistern, or even into the river directly, and lugged it home themselves.

Water was rarely drunk in London. It was often foul smelling and had a salty taste, especially if it came from the Thames. Sometimes people boiled it, which improved its taste somewhat, and used it to dilute wine. Otherwise, water was used mostly for cooking, cleaning, and, occasionally, for bathing.

# The Houses of London

*Much of what is known today of the details of daily life in Elizabethan times comes from the writings of William Harrison, a scholar who lived from 1534 to 1593. The following excerpt from Harrison's writings, found in R.E. Pritchard's* Shakespeare's England, *describes the planning and construction of some of the finer houses in and around London.*

The greatest part of our building in the cities and good towns of England consisteth only of timber, for as yet few of the houses of the commonality (except here and there in the West Country towns) are made of stone, although they may, in my opinion, in diverse places be builded so good cheap of one as of the other. In old time the houses of the Britons [early Englishmen] were slightly set up, with a few posts and many raddles [rails], the like whereof almost is to be seen in the . . . northern parts unto this day, where for lack of wood they are enforced to continue this ancient manner of building. . . . In plastering likewise of our fairest houses over our heads, we use to lay first a layer or two of white mortar tempered with hair, upon laths, which are nailed one by another (or sometimes upon reed or wicker, more dangerous for fire, and made fast here and there with sap-laths, for falling down) and finally cover all with the aforesaid plaster, which, beside the delectable whiteness of the stuff itself, is laid on so even and smoothly, as nothing, in my judgement, can be done with more exactness. The walls of our houses on the inner sides in like sort be either hanged with tapestry . . . or painted cloths.

*An illustration of a sixteenth-century timber-framed house.*

# Bathing, Jordans, and Privies

Bathing was not a priority for the Elizabethans. Even Queen Elizabeth, who was said to have a beautiful bathing room that had a huge tub and full-length mirrors on the wall, was said to have used it only once a month or so. Elizabethans, no matter what social class, were suspicious of full-body bathing. Any large tub took up valuable living space in a cramped home, and heating the amount of water necessary took far too long.

Thus, most Elizabethans rarely bathed. Instead, they washed their faces and hands in the morning and before eating. They used a basin and a wide-mouthed pitcher, called an ewer, and sometimes, but not always, a ball of soap. Soap was made by wives in many homes; they strained boiling water through wood ashes to make lye and then added animal fat. To try masking the rancid smell of the animal fat, some women added almond oil or musk to their soap.

Instead of toilets, the Elizabethans used chamber pots, which were often called jordans. These were portable containers, usually made of metal or clay, for holding human waste. Because the jordan was not attached to the floor or any plumbing apparatus, a special room was needed to accommodate it. The jordan was simply brought out when needed and was emptied afterwards by either a servant or the user, if there were no servants in the house.

Another form of the chamber pot was the closestool, which was merely a stool with a hole in it. It was surrounded by fabric on all sides, which concealed the chamber pot inside. These, too, were portable and could be carried from room to room in larger homes. Elizabeth had several closestools in her residences, and the royal attendant who emptied her chamber pot even had a title: groom of the stool.

Reportedly, the queen preferred closestools to the privy, a small room of its own with a permanent seat and a cesspit underneath. Many in the gentle class owned privies because, even though they were costly to maintain, they had the advantage of privacy for the user. However, the privy had a serious drawback, too: Because of the difficulty in cleaning the cesspit underneath, the room continually stank and tended to attract hordes of flies.

# Marketing

One of the most important aspects of maintaining a household was marketing. During Elizabethan times, London markets were held outdoors on Wednesday and Saturday mornings. Women, sometimes bringing children and servants, went from vendor to street stall to shops, buying things their families needed.

The old market area of the city was a wide street called Cheapside. From Cheapside ran dozens of narrow streets named for the wares they sold, such as Milk Street and Honey Lane. Fish could be purchased on Friday Street (so named for the long-standing church rule against eating meat on Fridays). These businesses thrived, although it was widely known that merchants were sometimes dishonest about the quality of their wares. One visitor to Cheapside at the time wrote sarcastically, "There are a great company of honest men in this place if all be gold that glitters. . . . Most of them have better faces than heart."[36]

Not far from Cheapside was St. Paul's Cathedral, once a Catholic church and in Elizabeth's day (since Catholicism had been banned) a large market area. Outside the cathedral were booksellers' stalls, where one could buy the newest play, joke book, or poetry volume for a penny or two. Shoppers who ventured into the area were taking a risk, however, for it was a place where beggars, idlers, pimps, and thieves congregated, often inside the cathedral itself. Says one historian, "Advertisements—some of them disreputable—covered the walls. Robberies were plotted and sexual liaisons arranged. Anything could be bought, sold, or hired."[37]

## Laundry

Saturday was also laundry and washing day for many women. Laundry was one of the most difficult chores wives and servants did, partly because of the lack of plumbing and because of the amount of time that washing clothes took.

Perhaps the difficulty of the chore was why most clothing—such as pants, coats, jackets, and outer shirts—was never washed; instead, it was cleaned off occasionally with a clothes brush. Only the clothing worn close to the body, such as

## Cleaning a Tablecloth

*In her book* The Pageant of Stuart England, *Elizabeth Burton relates a detailed set of instructions for cleaning a dirty tablecloth during the seventeenth century; these instructions were followed during Elizabethan times, too, and probably even earlier. Obviously, removing stains (if indeed this method did remove them) was a time-consuming effort.*

First, soak the cloth from Saturday to Monday in a thick green mixture of soft water and sheep's dung; only summer dung will do. From Monday to Wednesday, dip repeatedly into a pond or river. On Wednesday, beat out and leave to soak in pond or river until Thursday afternoon; then allow to dry. (Either the weather was better than it is now, or drying took place indoors.) Next day, put it into a tub, spread a buck sheet over it, make a thin paste of Dog's mercury [an acrid, foul-smelling herb that is poisonous to many animals] Mallow, Kecks, or Wormwood [various plants], spread this over the buck sheet, then pour strong boiling hot lye over the lot, cover and allow to stand overnight. By Friday it is ready to be spread out on the grass and watered all morning. Friday night, repeat the buck sheet process; do this again on Saturday. Saturday night, drop the cloth into lye and allow to soak until Monday morning. It is then ready to be laid out once more and watered every day with pond water until white enough!

underwear, was laundered. The garments were soaked in a mixture of soap, lye, and hot water for several hours. Afterward, the clothes would be beaten with wooden clubs, called beetles, and left to dry in the sun.

Sometimes clothes that were especially stained were cleaned with a recipe from the Roman times, which was a mixture of egg white, lye, salt, burnt alum, and an excretion from the liver of a bull, all rolled up in a ball. Occasionally, human urine was collected from chamber pots and used if lye was scarce. Although the urine may have removed some stains, it is not surprising that the mixture also left clothing smelling foul.

The Elizabethans' reputation for the foul smell of their clothing was widely reported by travelers to England. One visitor recalled being invited to dinner and noting that the napkins were dirty and the tablecloth looked "as if a sow had farrowed [given birth] on it."[38] Fortunately, however, there were more positive aspects of their daily lives for which the Elizabethans were famous.

# Elizabethan Fashion

Few aspects of Elizabethan culture are as recognizable today as the clothing of the era. Clothing was extremely important to both men and women of the day, and the most fashionable clothing was ornate and heavy, often featuring huge collars and long capes. The styles of clothing worn by men and women—of almost every rung of the social ladder—had changed a great deal from the styles of the previous generation.

## "With Pearls the Size of Beans"

The prosperity of England during Elizabeth's reign had a lot to do with the change in the style of clothing. The country was not at war, and many citizens earned better salaries than ever before. A fancy wardrobe was a way for a man and his family—even in the middle class—to announce to the world they had money.

Merchants and traders traveled far from home to find new materials, fabrics, jewels, and other things not found in England. From Italy they brought back thick velvets and intricate laces; from Germany they brought the smoothest linens the Elizabethans had ever seen. They brought silk and colorful embroidered fabric from Spain, and from Persia, India, and North America, merchants and traders brought all sorts of jewels, furs, and even feathers, which had not been seen in England before.

Elizabeth was pleased with the new fabrics and jewels that were brought into

*Queen Elizabeth dresses in elegant clothing for a portrait.*

the country, and she was quick to command her staff to incorporate these new items into her own wardrobe. One visitor to England in 1598 described the sixty-five-year-old queen as being dressed in clothing that was unbelievably fine: "She had in her ears two pearls, with very rich drops, . . . she had on a necklace of exceedingly fine jewels. . . . She was dressed in white silk, bordered with pearls the size of beans, and over it a mantle of black silk, shot with silver threads; her train was very long . . .

instead of a chain she had an oblong collar of gold and jewels."[39]

## Looking Elsewhere for Style

In addition to adding exciting new fabrics and gems to her wardrobe, Elizabeth sought new styles for her gowns. She strongly preferred the fashions of some other European countries over those that were typically available in England. Farthingales, the large hoopskirts, were a Spanish creation, and Elizabeth ordered her dressmakers to make her some of those. She also liked some French and Italian dress designs, and she ordered those, too.

She did have to be cautious about letting her preference for French designs be known, however, because England had recently fought a war with France, and relations between the countries were not warm. In 1566 she commanded her adviser to write to the English ambassador in Paris to find her a French tailor. In his letter, the queen's adviser suggested that the ambassador be discreet about hiring such a tailor: "The Queen's Majesty would [rather] have a tailor that had skill to make her apparel both after the Italian and French manner; . . . you might . . . obtain someone that serveth the French queen, without mentioning any manner of request in our queen's majesty's name."[40]

## Filtering Down to the Middle Class

Although certainly not a typical citizen of her time, Elizabeth had a remarkable impact on how many of her subjects dressed. For although it was obvious that no one could afford the same jeweled gowns that Elizabeth wore, there was a great demand from middle-class women that clothiers make gowns that they could afford in the style that Elizabeth was wearing. In this way, preferences from the queen and her court spread to the gentle class and then to the middle class.

These fashions were not comfortable; instead, the design gave the impression of stiffness and formality—a regal and sturdy presence rather than one of a working person. Though Elizabeth herself wore this type of clothing throughout the day, the middle-class women emulating her saved these garments for social events.

The look of these garments was striking. The clothes had the effect of flattening and narrowing a woman's body above the waist and at the same time increasing its size below the waist. The effect was accomplished in a number of ways, starting with the undergarments.

## "Puppets"

The bodice, which was a combination girdle and bra, was the foundation of the Elizabethan look. Women with servants who helped them dress had bodices that laced up the back; otherwise, bodices were front-lacing garments that fastened with a hook and eye. Bodices needed to be stiff to be effective; they were stiffened by whale bone, wood, or even bundles of dried reeds.

A new device that narrowed a woman's upper body even more was the busk. Busks were made from wood or whale bone and would fit over the woman's bust, flattening it.

Over the busk and bodice, women wore stiff, heavy dresses with padded, oversize sleeves that looked as though they belonged on someone three or four times the wearer's size. One observer, who did not agree that the effect of long

*An illustration depicts Elizabethan women wearing the fashions of the day.*

sleeves and a tiny upper body was at all pleasing on women, noted that the sleeves "hanging down to their skirts, trailing on the ground, and cast over their shoulders like cow tails" make women in these gowns "seem to be the smallest part of themselves, not . . . women of flesh and blood, but rather puppets . . . consisting of rags and [patches] compact together."[41]

## Goose-Turd Green and Puke Brown

To complete the effect, the Elizabethan woman exaggerated the size of her lower body with the farthingale hoopskirt. It, too, must have been very uncomfortable, for the skirt's shape was formed by a frame of wire or wooden hoops sewn inside. The hoops began just under the waist and increased in size down to the floor, forming a bell shape. Sometimes women put a padded roll around their waists to make the skirt tip up farther from their rear ends. These were aptly named "bum rolls" by the English, from the slang term "bum", for buttocks.

These gowns and skirts came in a variety of popular colors. The queen was by law the only person allowed to wear royal purple in those days because it was the official color of royalty; but all other colors were permitted. The various shades of the times have odd names by modern standards, but they were simply descriptive to Elizabethans. Some of the most common shades of gowns for women were pease porridge, horseflesh, puke brown, and goose-turd green. There was even a popu-

lar shade known as dead Spaniard beige, although the reason for the term is not clear today.

## "Like a Head on a Platter"

Another recognizable feature of Elizabethan formal clothing is the ruff, or ruffled collar. Collars for both men's and women's shirts changed dramatically during the Elizabethan era. The style evolved from a gathered neckline in shirts to a ruff sewn on the neckline. As the years went on, ruffs became larger and more pronounced, especially after starch became widely used in 1559.

Three ruffs were piled on top of one another, and all were pleated. Some were so large that they extended nine inches from the neck, framing the face of the wearer to such a degree that it almost seemed as though the head were separate from the body. In Ben Jonson's play *The Alchemist*, written just after Elizabeth's death, a character remarks, "He looks in that deep ruff like a head on a platter."[42]

Ruffs were fashionable but impractical. Maintaining a collar took a great deal of work. Launderers worked overtime spreading a paste of starch on it and then drying each flute of the ruff individually over a fire. Ruffs also sagged in rainy or humid weather and made eating difficult. To help with the second problem, say historians, a London silversmith created a special spoon with an extra-long handle.

# Men's Fashions

Elizabethan fashion fads were not limited to women's clothes. Men's clothing changed a great deal, too. A "peasecod belly" was one popular look among the upper and middle classes. It was achieved by wearing a close-fitting jacket, called a doublet, that was heavily padded in the front. The padding was usually bombast,

*Queen Elizabeth poses in a gown with a pronounced ruffled collar.*

a stuffing made of wool, horsehair, linen fibers, or even bran. One observer of the day witnessed a man whose doublet contained so much bombast that he seemed to be "carrying the whole contents of his bed and his table linen."[43]

Garments for men's lower bodies also changed during Elizabeth's reign. Early during the sixteenth century, most men wore loose-fitting wool tights, called long hose. There was no elastic in those days, so the tights were laced to the doublet as a way of keeping them up. But by 1550, well-dressed men were wearing something on top of the long hose. It was a pair of puffy, padded shorts, called trunk hose, which one historian says was "stuffed to the shape of a plump inverted heart."[44]

Men's trunk hose and doublets, as well as women's gowns and skirts, were frequently slashed vertically, leaving one-inch gashes all over the garments. The purpose of slashing was to show a contrasting color or fabric underneath.

## The Length Tells All

For men, outer garments—jackets and cloaks—told their social class. A common laborer or servant wore a jerkin, a jacket made of wool. It was

47

# The Devil's Cartwheel

*One of the strangest fashions of the Elizabethan time was the ruff, a cumbersome collar worn by both men and women. Because wearing the ruff was often a sign of vanity among the upper classes and social climbing among the middle class, the collar was harshly criticized by one Puritan writer of the day, who called them "cartwheels of the Devil's chariot." His remarks are included in* Shakespeare's England, *by R.E. Pritchard.*

[People today] have great and monstrous ruffs, made of cambric, holland [linen], lawn or else of some other the finest cloth that can be got for money, whereof some be a quarter of a yard, yea, some more, very few less, so that they stand a full quarter of a yard (and more) from their necks, hanging over their shoulder points, instead of a veil. But if Aeolus [mythical god of the wind] with his blasts or Neptune [mythical god of the sea] with his storms, chance to hit upon the crazy bark of their bruised ruffs, then they go flip flap in the wind like rags flying abroad, and lie upon their shoulders like the dishcloth of a slut. But wot [know] you what? The Devil, as he in the fullness of his malice first invented these great ruffs, so hath he now found out also two great stays to bear up and maintain this his kingdom of great ruffs (for the Devil is king and prince over all the children of pride). The one arch or pillar whereby his kingdom of great ruffs is underpropped is a certain kind of liquid matter which they call Starch, wherein the Devil has willed them to wash and dive his ruffs well, which when they be dry will then stand stiff and inflexible about their necks.

*The ornate Elizabethan ruffled collar was thought by Puritans to be the creation of the devil.*

loose fitting and knee length, which allowed him to work without the garment getting in his way. He could fasten the jerkin at the waist with a belt.

Middle-class men, who had less physical jobs, such as being a teacher, physician, merchant, or lawyer, were easily identified by their long robes. The robes came to their ankles and the sleeves to their elbows—a style that would be impractical for lower-class workers.

Gentlemen and members of the nobility wore shorter coats than the middle class. They spent a lot of time outdoors riding and hunting, and short coats were far more practical on horseback. Unlike the laborer's jerkin, the coat of the upper classes was velvet or fur lined and often embroidered.

## Ape of All Nations?

People visiting England during the reign of Elizabeth were often amazed at the clothes people wore—not just the queen and the nobility, but the middle classes and even the commoners. Although lacking the jewels, furs, and embroidery of the high-priced items, the clothing of the ordinary people seemed excessively fashionable, too. In 1596 one English writer poked fun at farmers and laborers, who had never cared before about fashion but had taken a sudden interest: "The Ploughman that in times past was contented in russet must nowadays have his doublet of the fashion with wide cuts, his garters of fine silk of [Spain] to met his Sis on Sunday; the farmer that was contented in times past

*This portrait of William Shakespeare depicts the embroidered short coat worn by the Elizabethan nobility.*

with his russet frock and mockado sleeves now sells a cow against Easter to buy him silken gear."[45]

But there was harsh criticism, too, concerning the English fashion. Some other Europeans ridiculed the English for stealing the designs, calling them "the apes of all nations."[46] Having no style of their own, claimed the critics, the English had to borrow the most interesting and unusual ideas from other countries and passed the hodgepodge off as Elizabethan fashion.

But the harshest critics were English themselves—often conservative churchmen who believed that the attention Londoners were paying to fashion showed how vain and self-serving they were becoming. "Oh," laments William Harrison, "how much cost is bestowed nowadays upon our bodies, and how little upon our souls! How many suits of apparel hath the one, and how little furniture hath the other!" And he decries the fashions as making it difficult to tell men from women:

> What should I say of their doublets . . . full of jags and cuts, and sleeves of sundry [various] colors? Their galligaskins [loose skirts] to bear out their bums and make their attire to fit plum round . . . about them. Their farthingales and diversely coloured nether stocks of silk, jersey, and such like, whereby their bodies are rather deformed than commended. . . . Thus it is now come to pass, that women are become men, and men transformed into monsters.[47]

## As Pale as Skin Can Be

Had critics been aware of how much time and preparation went into other aspects of style—especially makeup—they probably would have had much to say about that, too. A beautiful woman in Elizabethan times was one with very white skin; a white complexion was the mark of wealth, nobility, and delicacy. But naturally white skin was exceptionally rare, so women who wanted the look had to use a number of creams and chemicals to achieve it.

The best whitener was called ceruse. Ceruse was made by steeping lead bars in either urine or vinegar and then scraping off the white flakes that resulted and making them into a paste. A woman spread the paste onto her face and bosom if she planned to wear a gown without a ruff.

Because chemists made ceruse, it tended to be expensive. However, there were homemade whiteners that ordinary housewives could use. Some women chose to bleach their skin, using a mixture of sulfur and borax. Another, often used by country women, was made from grinding the jawbone of a hog and mixing the powder with poppy oil.

Women applied the whiteners thickly, making sure to cover acne, freckles, or scars left from smallpox. One observer recalled seeing a woman whose makeup was nearly two inches thick. Another noted that women used so much ceruse at one time that "a man might easily cut off a curd or cheesecake from either of their cheeks."[48]

## "You'll Mar It If You Kiss It"

After the whitening was done, a woman would go on to the next stage of her makeup. She used a pencil to draw blue veins on the exposed skin of her chest and neck. This was meant to give the illusion that her skin was now so transparent the veins were showing. She then applied blackening powder to her eyelids and a red paste known as vermilion to her lips, as well as a spot on each cheek.

# Fickleness and Folly

*Elizabethan essayist William Harrison was quite critical in his descriptions of the way people dressed, no matter what their social class. Harrison insisted that people spent far too much money and time on their attire as well as on their jewelry and other accessories. His comments are included in Allardyce Nicoll's The Elizabethans.*

The fantastical folly of our nation, even from the courtier to the carter, is such that no form of apparel liketh us longer than the first garment is in the wearing, if it continue so long and be not laid aside to receive some other trinket newly devised by the fickle-headed tailors, who covet to have several tricks in cutting, thereby to draw fond customers to more expense of money.

Such is our mutability [quickness to change] that today there is none to the Spanish guise, tomorrow the French toys are most fine and delectable, ere long no such apparel as that which is after the high Almaine [German] fashion; by and by the Turkish manner is generally best liked of, otherwise the Morisco [Moorish] gowns, the Barbarian sleeves and the short French breeches make such a comely vesture [handsome outfit] that, except it were a dog in a doublet, you shall not see any so disguised as are my countrymen of England. And as these fashions are diverse, so likewise it is a world to see the costliness and the curiosity, the excess and the vanity, the pomp and the bravery, the change and the variety, and finally the fickleness and the folly that is in all degrees, insomuch that nothing is more constant in England than inconstancy of attire.

Once she had achieved the look she wanted, a woman brushed on a protective glaze of egg white. This helped keep the ceruse and other pastes from smearing. But the glaze was not foolproof. A character in William Shakespeare's play *The Winter's Tale* recognizes this when she cautions Leontes against kissing Hermione:

forbear
The ruddiness on her lip is wet

You'll mar it if you kiss it; stain your own
With oily painting.[49]

Because makeup in Elizabethan times was so time-consuming to apply, women did not take it with them when they went out for the evening. Instead, they "saved" their faces by wearing a leather or cloth mask with tiny holes to see through while en route to their destination. The queen's mask had glass in it, so she did not have to peer through holes in the leather.

*The reddish gold of Queen Elizabeth's curls was the most fashionable hair color of the day.*

## Hair

Fashion trends included hair, too—for women as well as men. Reddish gold became the most fashionable hair color, since that was Elizabeth's color. People used combinations of all sorts of chemicals and extracts, including sulfur, lime, water drawn from honey, and even apple peelings to achieve this color. Very rich women even sprinkled their hair (and rich men, their beards) with gold dust. Some, concerned that the mixtures they were using would bleach their hair too light, used a strange mixture of oil, ashes, and earthworms, which would lighten the hair for just a few hours.

A few of the formulas involved more than simply mixing and applying the dye to one's hair. Some required long periods of drying and rinsing, as this 1558 recipe for red gold hair explains: "To make the hair yellow as gold: Take the rind or scrapings of rhubarb, and steep it in white wine, or in clear lye, and after you have washed your head with it, you shall wet your hairs with a Spoonge or some other cloth, and let them drie by the fire, or in the sun; after this wet them and dry them again."[50]

Elizabethan women also loved the look of a high forehead, for it seemed to them aristocratic and regal. They did several things to achieve this look. They spent a great deal of time plucking their eyebrows to a fine, thin line. They wore their hair piled high on their heads, and they often plucked or shaved an inch or two of hair to create the look of a high forehead.

## "Like a Spanish Mule"

Although Elizabethan women felt beautiful after using these cosmetics and dyes on their faces and hair, they were also doing irreparable damage to themselves. Ceruse, the whitening cosmetic, was one of the most dangerous. Its high lead content was toxic, and as the years went by, users of ceruse often suffered open sores, baldness, and mental deficiency. A lifetime of using it did damage to Elizabeth's skin; according to historians, she banned mirrors from her rooms late in her life so that she did not have to look at her ravaged skin.

Vermilion caused unpleasant side effects, too, especially sores and other skin damage. One Italian observer noted how ironic it was that women used the substance to look more beautiful, but that it eventually made them ugly:

Such women as use it about their face, have always black teeth, standing far out of their gums like a Spanish mule; an offensive breath, with a face half scorched and an unclean complexion. All which pro-

ceed from the nature of [the cosmetic]. So that simple women thinking to grow more beautiful, become disfigured, hastening old age before the time.[51]

Most of these effects were not mysteries. Elizabethan women knew some of the damage they were doing to themselves, yet they continued to use such chemicals. Researchers speculate that it may have been an acceptable choice in a time when life could be very difficult. As one historian notes, "In a world where life tended to be short and health fleeting, one's physical well-being was less compelling than momentary beauty."[52]

# At the Table

Just as visitors to London during Elizabeth's reign found the people far better dressed than citizens in most other countries, they also thought the English were better fed. "They take great pleasure in having a quantity of excellent victuals," a traveler from Venice notes, "and also in remaining a long time at table."[53]

One Englishman of the time admitted that he and his countrymen tended to eat more, but he explained that it was because of England's geographic location. "Our region lying near unto the North," he writes, "doth cause the heats of our stomachs to be of somewhat greater force, therefore our bodies do crave a little more ample nourish-ment than the inhabitants of the hotter regions."[54]

## The Three Food Groups

No matter what the reason, it is true that people in Elizabethan London tended to be well fed. Although there was a difference between the selection of foods on a wealthy man's table and that of a commoner, all Elizabethans got most of their daily calories from three foods: meat, bread, and beer.

The selection of meats was probably what set the English diet apart from that of other Europeans of the sixteenth century. Wealthy families ate a great variety of meats—usually six or seven meat dishes at a single meal. In fact, one essayist of the time notes that of the fifteen courses thought necessary for a small dinner party, thirteen of them were meat dishes, including pork with mustard, boiled beef, roasted beef, roasted cow's tongue, turkey, swan, venison, and kid (young goat). Since many wealthy people had hunting privileges in London, various game meats such as deer, rabbit, and pheasant often appeared on their tables.

For most Londoners, however, mutton and pork were the most readily available meats; chickens and geese were common, too. The middle class dined on these meats most of the year, choosing to imitate the lavish meals of the wealthy only occasionally. These would be feasts, such as parties for friends or perhaps a way of celebrating a special event or holiday. In poor families, meat was served only once or twice a week, and often that was a fatty cut of salted pork.

## Fish Laws

Fish was also eaten frequently in Elizabethan London. The reason is not that people were especially fond of it, or that they preferred it over meat, but that there were laws requiring them to eat it. When King Henry VIII replaced Catholicism with the Protestant Church of England in 1530, England's fishing industry suffered. The industry had relied heavily on

*A kitchen servant removes the entrails of a cow, while another stirs a cauldron over an open fire. Elizabethans enjoyed a more nourishing diet than most of their European neighbors.*

the Catholic ban on meat on Fridays and during Lent, for on those days people had eaten fish.

The Church of England had no such bans, though, and when fishermen in coastal towns began losing money, laws were passed making the eating of fish compulsory on Fridays, Saturdays, and all during Lent. It was a political law, rather than a religious one, and it helped the fishermen survive. It also provided people with a little more variety in their diet.

In London, stalls on Friday Street sold all sorts of fresh (or somewhat fresh) fish, and eels, pike, salmon, and tench were common. Some housewives made eel pie, which was considered a great delicacy. However, the most common fish sold was stockfish, a form of dried codfish that required a great amount of energy to prepare. Because it dried into a rock-hard brick, stockfish needed to be hammered with a wooden mallet and soaked for hours in warm water before it could be eaten. It was cheap, though, so the lower classes ate a great deal of it.

## Manchet and Other Breads

Bread was another staple of the Elizabethan diet, and it was served in some form at every meal. Pottage, also made from grain, was similar to oatmeal, and it was frequently served in the homes of every social class. Sometimes a little meat would be added or, in wealthy homes, almonds, cinnamon, and ginger.

Everyone ate bread, but it differed in texture and ingredients. Wheat flour was considered best for bread, but wheat was expensive. A lower-class housewife might make bread from other grains, such as barley, rye, or a combination of grains. On the low end of the spectrum was horse bread, made of ground-up beans. Just as its name suggests, it was made to feed horses, although poor Londoners would eat it if times were tight.

Wealthy Elizabethans ate brown bread from wheat flour most of the time, and they were served white bread occasionally. White bread was more difficult to make since the flour had to be sifted through a linen cloth to remove the outer layer of wheat. White bread was not nearly as filling as brown, either; whereas a loaf of brown bread weighed about six pounds, a white loaf weighed only about two. Even so, say historians, wealthy people ate it because a man who served white bread at his table was demonstrating that he could afford to eat a lot of other foods, too.

## Beer (and Ale) for Everyone

The English of the sixteenth century had few choices of beverages. The smell and look of water was often suspicious to the Elizabethans, and few were willing to do more than cook or clean with it—drinking it had little appeal. "Water," advised one medical expert of the time, "is not wholesome sole by itself for an Englishman."[55]

Milk was not as plentiful then; cows did not give as much milk as they do in modern times. Almost all of the milk that they did produce was used for making butter and cheese, which Elizabethans found to be more important to their diet. (Some country people did drink whey, which is the liquid part left over after making cheese.) Coffee was not drunk, nor had England become a nation of tea drinkers; tea was not introduced until the mid-1600s, and then it was so expensive that only wealthy people could afford it. The Elizabethans enjoyed wine, but because it had to be imported, it was too expensive for everyday consumption.

What people of all ages did drink was beer or ale. Ale, somewhat stronger than beer, was fairly inexpensive to make and people liked the taste; however, it did not keep well in warm weather. Beer, on the other hand, did not spoil as easily, so Elizabethans brewed beer in large quantities and stored it. Because it was made in such large amounts, it was ridiculously cheap; William Harrison reported that his wife and her helpers made two hundred gallons of beer, at a cost of about a penny a gallon.

## The Potato of America and Sallats

During the time of Elizabeth's father, Henry VIII, who ruled between 1509 and 1547, vegetables were rarely eaten. The king believed they were "a food more fit for hogs and savage beasts."[56] By Elizabeth's day, however, people were beginning to see "herbs," as vegetables were called then, as useful in providing more variety to a meal. Country people added them to pottage and especially

An illustration depicts a festive scene in an Elizabethan tavern.

enjoyed onions, turnips, carrots, beans, and cabbage.

One vegetable that became quite popular during this era was the potato, or as it was called then, the potato of America, since it was imported from the New World. Elizabethans served potatoes in a number of ways—roasted in hot coals, with butter, oil, or vinegar—and found them delicious. It was not always easy to get potatoes at first, so it was a mark of distinction for a host to serve them.

A common way for the Elizabethans to eat many different vegetables was in salads, or "sallats." Experts of the day particularly urged people to eat a lot of lettuce in their sallats, although not because

*A portrait of King Henry VIII, who believed vegetables to be unfit for human consumption.*

The Elizabethans loved sweet foods, so it was not suprising that sugar was a prized commodity. In fact, the extent of people's use of refined sugar was a good indication of their social class. Poor families could not afford refined sugar; they used fruit and honey as sweeteners. The middle classes bought sugar and used it only for special feasts, such as Christmas, for baking and making candy and jelly. The upper classes, though, were able to afford so much sugar that they made a paste of it and sculpted it to make banquet decorations. One man described a particularly elegant display of more than one hundred such sculptures at an ambassadors' dinner:

> The wonder was no less that it was worthy indeed. There were castles with images in the same, Paul's Church [St. Paul's Cathedral] and steeple in proportion for the quantity. . . . There were beasts, birds, fowls of [various] kinds and personages, most lively made . . . some fighting, as it were with swords, some with guns and crossbows, some vaulting and leaping, some dancing with ladies.[58]

of any nutritional benefits. One wrote that lettuce was an especially good way to end the meal because it could keep "away drunkenness which cometh by the wine; and that is by reason that it stayeth the vapours from rising up into the head."[57]

## Fruit and Sugar

Although Elizabethans were just learning to enjoy vegetables, fruit had always been popular. People were less apt to eat raw fruits because for centuries physicians had warned them that uncooked fruits caused fevers. Cherries, pears, apricots, and plums were common in England and were cooked and used in pies, cakes, jellies, and tarts.

## Preserving Food

No matter what one's social rank, however, the preservation of food was a problem. There was no refrigeration, and the bugs and rodents in households meant that food had to be stored very carefully. Meat and fish were often smoked or salted, which meant that they could go longer without spoiling. Some fruits, such as apricots and plums, were dried or made into preserves for the same reason.

Containers played an important role in keeping food from spoiling, too. Wooden barrels held salted fish, beer, and dried fruit so that they would not fall victim to insects and other vermin. A gallipot, a clay jar with straight sides, was especially useful. Because it was airtight, short-lived foods like butter and milk could last longer in it. Some cooks even used a pie crust to provide an airtight seal over meat, keeping it fresh for a few days.

# Little Food Wasted

*In his "Description of England," written in 1587, William Harrison describes in great detail the amounts of food on a wealthy man's table. He explains that while much of the food is not eaten (especially the vast varieties of meat dishes) none of it is wasted. This excerpt is included in* Shakespeare's England: Life in Elizabethan and Jacobean Times, *edited by R.E. Pritchard.*

In numbers of dishes and changes of meat, the nobility of England (whose cooks are for the most part musical-headed Frenchmen and strangers) do most exceed, sith [since] there is no day in manner that passeth over their heads wherein they have not only beef, mutton, veal, lamb, kid [goat], pork, coney [rabbit], capon [chicken], pig, or so many of these as the season yieldeth, but also some portion of the red or fallow deer, beside great variety of fish and wildfowl, and thereto sundry [various] other delicates wherein the sweet hand of the seafaring Portingale [Portugal] is not wanting. So that for a man to dine with one of them and to taste of every dish that standeth before him (which few use to do, but each one feedeth upon that him best liketh for the time) is rather to yield unto a conspiracy with a great deal of meat for the speedy suppression of natural health than to satisfy himself with a competent repast [meal] to sustain his body withal. But as this large feeding is not seen in their guests, no more is it in their own persons, for sith they have daily much resort unto their tables . . . and thereto retain great numbers of servants, it is very requisite [important] and expedient in them to be somewhat plentiful in this behalf. . . .

The chief part likewise of their daily provision is brought in before them . . . and placed on their tables, whereof when they have taken what it pleaseth them, the rest is reserved, and afterward sent down to their serving men and waiters, who feed thereon in like sort with convenient moderation, their reversion also being bestowed upon the poor, which lie ready at their gates in great numbers.

Although most of these methods make sense, there are a few preservation methods that seem extremely odd. One was a method of preserving cherries for fresh Christmas tarts by putting them in a barrel of hay placed inside a feather mattress.

From the recipes for tainted meat that remain from Elizabethan times, it is plain that their systems of preserving food were not always successful. Foods spoiled often, but people were unwilling to waste it. Because of this, the Elizabethans came up with various ways to make spoiled meats, fruits, and other foods bearable. Some of these suggestions called for heavy use of spices to mask the taste, but others were more involved.

One recipe, offered by sixteenth-century gardening and cooking authority Sir Hugh Platt, was a way to salvage venison that had become so spoiled that it had turned green: "First remove the bones, wrap [the meat] in an old coarse-textured cloth, dig a hole in the earth three foot deep and bury the venison for from twelve to twenty hours, according to the degree of greenness. When dug up, it will be found to be sweet enough to eat."[59]

## Hot Kitchens and Naked Chefs

In addition to a collection of foods in storage jars and barrels, Elizabethan kitchens contained a fireplace and one or more ovens, which were central to all of the home's cooking needs. The fireplace burned wood, straw, peat, or coal, and its heat made the entire kitchen (or, when the kitchen was inside the home, the entire house) so hot that it was almost intolerable. One writer of the time describes the kitchen of a wealthy home

*Two pastry chefs roll dough while a third bakes the confections using the wood-burning oven typical of the Elizabethan kitchen.*

as a kind of hell, with "the Divell in it, where [the cook's] meate and he fry together."[60] Kitchens in Elizabeth's day had not changed at all from those of her father's reign, where the heat was reportedly so intense that cooks and other kitchen staff worked in the nude.

To use fuel efficiently, cooks cooked several things at once, using a system of hooks and chains to hold various pots. The chains could be adjusted to move the pots up and down, depending on the temperature needed to cook the particular food. Some pots had legs, and could be set directly on the fire to boil.

Meat was not put into pots but was usually roasted on a long metal rod, called a spit. A pan under the meat caught the juices, which could be used to make gravy. Spit-roasting was considered the best way of ensuring tender meat, and visitors from other nations, where meat was fried or boiled, were impressed by the taste. One who visited early in 1605 noted, "English cooks in comparison with other nations are most commended for roasted meat."[61]

## Turnspit Dogs

But the process of spit-roasting was difficult; to keep the meat from burning, it was necessary to turn it often. In previous generations, the job sometimes fell to a servant or, in lower-class families, to one of the children. It was hot work, and by the mid-1500s people had found ways to avoid the job by giving it to certain small dogs, known as turnspits.

People attached small treadmills to the spit, and as the dogs would run, a wheel would turn the spit. It was hard on the animals. The wheel was small and close to the hot fire. To keep the dogs moving quickly, a kitchen worker occasionally put a hot coal by their back feet. The dogs ran on their wheels for hours at a time; when one dish was done, a cook often put another cut of meat on the spit, and the turnspit began again. The phrase "It's a dog's life" supposedly originated from people's observing the difficult existence of the turnspit.

Turnspits were not particularly handsome dogs; they have been described as having long bodies, strong but bowed legs, and a rather suspicious, uneasy look about them. One historian notes that they were "the most wretched of creatures, dejected and abused, [and were] kicked around the kitchen."[62] Turnspits were gradually replaced by an automatic turning mechanism during the seventeenth century, and the breed died out.

## Sitting Down to a Meal

As the housewife finished preparing the food for the meal, another family member—usually one of the children—set the table for the meal. A white linen cloth was spread over the large table, and tableware was put out. The arrangement of items on the dinner table looked only somewhat different from a modern table.

For one thing, utensils were sparse. Each person had a spoon, usually made of horn or pewter; it was the same spoon that he or she used at every meal each day. Spoons were considered a very personal item and were often given as a present at a child's christening or birthday. One's spoon was commonly kept in a leather case between meals.

Knives also were common; the amount of meat eaten at a single meal made them crucial. Many guests brought their own knives to the table. In fact, there were rules of etiquette about having one's knife in a fit condition to use at a table. One rule warned, "When ye be set, keep your own knife clean and sharp, that so ye may carve honestly your own meat."[63]

One utensil that the Elizabethans did not use was a fork, in fact, most had never seen one. In some wealthy homes, forks were occasionally used to steady a cut of meat as it was being carved, but they were never put in one's mouth. Using a fork as an eating utensil was fashionable only in Italy during the sixteenth century; in England, the fork was not widely used until the eighteenth century. Some considered it effeminate, and others believed it signaled godlessness. "God in his wisdom has provided man with natural forks," wrote one critic, "it is considered impious to substitute them by metallic artificial forks when eating."[64]

## Voiders and Trenchers

In addition to knives and spoons, each place was set with a trencher, which was a square wooden plate about the size of a modern salad plate. A trencher was made of wood in a commoner's house, and in poor families trenchers were created by scooping out dry old loaves of bread. In middle-class homes,

## "A Little Forke"

*Using a fork as an eating utensil seemed odd to the Elizabethans, and it was one of the strangest customs an English traveler noted among the Italians during the early seventeenth century. This record from a traveler's journal is included in* Food and Feast in Tudor England, *by Alison Sim.*

I observed a custom in all those Italian Cities and Townes through which I passed, that is not used in any other country that I saw in my travels, neithyer doe I thinke that any other nation of Chritendome [Christianity] doth use it, but only Italy. The Italian and also most strangers that are commorant [residing] in Italy do alwaies at their meales use a little forke when they cut their meate. For while with their knife which they hold in one hande they cut the meate out of the dish, they fasten their forke, which they hold in their other hand upon the same dish, so that whatsoever he be that sitting in the company of any others at meate, should unadvisedly touch the dish of meate with his fingers, from which at all the table doe cut, he will give occasion of offence unto the company, as having transgressed the lawes of good manners in so much that for his error he shall be at the least brow beaten, if not reprehended in wordes. . . . The reason of this curiosity is, because the Italian cannot by any means indure to have his dish touched with fingers, feeling all men's fingers are not alike cleane.

however, pewter and even silver trenchers were common during Elizabeth's reign.

There was another plate, larger than the trencher, that was set out on the table, too. It was called a voider, and it was used to hold bones, shells, or pieces of fat that could not be eaten. Voiders were shared by several people at the table; a small family of four might use just one, but a large group might need several. In addition to voiders, there were a number of communal plates—dishes and platters from which several people took food. Goblets and other drinking glasses were shared by two people and were set between places.

A salt box, or salt cellar, was put on the table, too. Salt was extremely important to Elizabethans, not only because it made their food taste better but also because it was very expensive. The salt cellar was always placed in front of the most important person at the table, most often the man of the house. A salt cellar might be silver or pewter, and it was frequently the most expensive piece of tableware a family owned.

## "Wipe Your Mouth Before You Drink"

With the numbers of people sharing dishes, good manners were considered very important. It would be rude, for example, for a person to put a bone he had chewed back onto a serving plate instead of onto a voider.

One important rule was that people should not put their knives in their mouths. Knives should be used to spear food from a communal dish, but once on one's trencher, the food was supposed to be eaten with the fingers. There was one unexplainable exception, however, as etiquette expert Hannah Woolley noted at the time: "Put not your Knife to your mouth, unless it be to eat an Egge."[65]

Besides limiting people's use of knives at the table, Elizabethan etiquette demanded a certain protocol involving napkins, too. A man was to drape his napkin over his left shoulder or his left forearm, and a woman was supposed to keep her napkin in her lap. And because people often shared drinking glasses, it was important to keep using the napkin throughout the meal. One often-repeated rule was to "wipe your mouth before you drink, lest it foul the edges of the cup, and keep your fingers, your lips, and your chin clean if you would win a good name."[66]

Even though many Elizabethan rules are similar to those of today, historians admit that a few aspects of their dining etiquette would horrify modern people. For example, it was permissable to spit while sitting at the table, although it was not good manners to do so loudly. Also, notes one historian, "You were . . . advised to wipe your hand on your clothes if you had to blow your nose so that other people did not have to see the results."[67] Even so, the rules of dining etiquette served the same purpose for Elizabethans as modern dining etiquette: It establishes a pleasant atmosphere for family and/or friends to share meals together.

# "Lord, Have Mercy upon London"

People during the Elizabethan era—especially in London—had a surprisingly short life expectancy. A baby born during this time was likely to live only about forty-eight years. There were many reasons for people's lives ending so young, including disease, accidents, a lack of medical understanding by physicians of the day, and, especially in London, dreadfully unsanitary conditions.

## Overcrowding and Filth

Much of the problem of sanitation stemmed from overcrowding. Too many people were living in a very small area of London. Poor people, often twenty or more, crowded into rooms that should have housed only four or five. More peo-

ple came to the city from the country, lured by the idea of a good job or a more interesting life than farming provided. New families, finding that housing was expensive, might simply move in with relatives in an already-crowded tenement.

By 1596 city officials had been warned by health experts of the negative effects and health hazards caused by the "great number of dissolute, loose, and insolent people harboured in such and the like noisome and disorderly houses, as namely poor cottages, and habitations of beggars and people without trade, stables, inns, alehouses, taverns, [and] garden-houses converted to dwellings."[68] In response, city officials attempted to limit the numbers of people in poor areas, but they had little success.

Even without the overcrowded conditions, however, the streets were a disaster. This was due in large measure to the lack of an efficient system of garbage and waste removal. In many sections of the city, people did not dispose of waste in nearby cesspits, or sewage dumping areas, as they were supposed to. Instead, many people poured out the contents of their chamber pots onto the street below, occasionally dousing an unlucky passerby with filth.

## Blood and Guts

People walking on the street should not have considered themselves lucky just by avoiding being hit with human waste, however. There were plenty of other things on the street that were hazardous to their health, and most of them could be found by smell alone. For instance, many citizens complained of the puddles of blood on the streets. It was a nuisance, disgusting to look at, and gave off a vile stench during warm weather.

Some of the blood was human, having been thrown out of a surgeon's office after a session of bloodletting. Most of it, however, was animal blood, usually from the butcher shops or slaughterhouses that were located in some residential areas. In 1603 physician Thomas Lodge urged that the city slaughterhouses be eliminated and instead "placed in some remote and convenient place neere unto the river of the Thames, to the end that the bloud and garbige of the beasts that are killed may be washed away with the tide."[69] Lodge's suggestion was ignored, and blood and entrails continued to pile up on the city's streets, fouling the air and annoying pedestrians.

## Rakers

Officials tried to respond to the problem by coming up with a system of waste removal. First, citizens were asked to be responsible for the areas in front of their homes by sweeping refuse into piles. This should be done, urged officials, both early in the morning and in the evening, after 8:00 P.M.

*Because Elizabethan London lacked an efficient sanitation system, the streets were filthy and unhealthy.*

Three times a week, a worker known as a raker blew a horn early in the morning, reminding people to bring down any other garbage they had and put it in a pile near their doorways. The raker gathered the garbage and took it away. He also cleaned off the streets so flies and other insects were not attracted by the residue of blood, human waste, and so on.

The system's flaw was the carelessness of London's citizens. There were some who were responsible, like a character in *The Shoemaker's Holiday* (a popular play of the era) who daily ordered his servants to "sweepe me these kennels, that the noysome stench offende not the nose of my neighbors."[70] However, many simply ignored the raker's horn, preferring to simply use the streets as their garbage dump.

# Contaminated Water

People's carelessness affected the water in and around the city, too. The ditch, a deep man-made defense that had been built to circle the city many centuries before, was well cared for at one time. It was cleaned and scoured on a regular basis. There were even fish within the ditch, say historians. However, it was neglected, and by the time Elizabeth came to the throne, the ditch was foul smelling and filthy, with garbage piled high around it.

The Thames, too, was contaminated. Craftsmen and housewives poured lye and other chemicals into the river after making soap or tanning hides. As a result, the water became foul, and the poisons began killing some of the fish. As with the problems with garbage in city streets, ordinances were passed making it illegal to dump rubbish or other waste in the Thames. Just as with the street ordinance, however, the problem worsened. All sorts of dumping went on, and citizens were shocked to see the variety of things that washed up on the river's banks, including the remains of animals killed in the city. The stench became so strong that in 1603 workers were offered money "for gathering of dogs and other noisome things out of the River of Thames and burying them."[71]

# Spittle, Vomit, and Dental Hygiene

There were health hazards in most citizens' homes, too. The straw-covered floors in many homes disgusted visitors, who saw that the straw not only attracted rats and mice but also stank. Dutch scholar Erasmus noted the variety of matter causing the smell: "The floors are made of clay and are covered with layers of rushes, constantly replenished, so that the bottom layer remains for twenty years harbouring spittle, vomit, the urine of dogs and men, the dregs of beer, the remains of fish, and other nameless filth."[72]

Personal hygiene was also poor. People did not brush their teeth; instead, they would rub them occasionally with a cloth or wash their mouths with one of many popular advertised remedies. In a 1602 book called *"Delightes for Ladies*, readers were provided with a surefire method of keeping the teeth "both white and sound." First, the

*A photo of an African civet, a species whose musk served as the fixative for a popular Elizabethan perfume.*

author writes, "take a quart of honey, as much vinegar, and half so much white wine, boil them together and wash your teeth therewith now and then."[73] Another recommendation involved burning the heads of mice which made "an excellent powder for the scouring and cleansing of the teeth."[74] It is not surprising, with honey and mouse skulls as prime ingredients in people's tooth care, that most Elizabethans had lost several teeth to decay by age sixteen, and to find an adult of forty with more than ten or eleven teeth was a rarity.

## Little Soap, but Lots of Perfume

Since most of the soap in Elizabethan households was used for laundry, not for bathing, people tended to smell bad. It was not that people then did not notice unpleasant odors; rather, they dealt with their effect instead of their cause.

In modern society, it is understood that bacteria on skin, combined with the moisture of perspiration, causes odor. However, since bacteria was an unknown concept during the sixteenth century,

# "Excluding Quacks"

*Perhaps because so much about sickness was not understood during the sixteenth century, phony healers, called "quacks," abounded. They promised cures for a price, and many desperate people were willing to pay. Physicians and surgeons, angry at the false hope the quacks offered (and at the loss of business for themselves) spent a great deal of time and energy trying to outlaw the quacks, as historian Penry Williams explains in his book,* Life in Tudor England.

Both physicians and surgeons were much occupied, as they are today, with excluding quacks and interlopers. . . . The College of Physicians was founded to keep out of medical practice "common arificers, as smiths, weavers, and women who boldly and customarily take upon themselves great cures . . . in which they use sorcery and apply medicines very noyous [disagreeable]." Considering the scale of the physicians' fees, it is not surprising that people flocked to the quacks, attracted by advertisements like this: "If any man, woman, or child, be sick or would be let blood, or be diseased with any manner of inward or outward griefs, as all manner of agues [chills] or fevers, pleurisies [respiratory infections], colic, stone, strangulation . . . let them resort to the Saracen's Head in the East Lane and they shall have remedy by me." Clearly all the regulations of the physicians were inadequate to suppress these charlatans [fakes]. . . . One surgeon angrily listed the quacks who claimed to practise his craft: "Now-a-days, it is apparent to see how tinkers, tooth-drawers, peddlars, ostlers [horse tenders], carters, porters, men, bawds, witches, conjurors, soothsayers, and sow-gelders, rogues, rat-catchers . . . daily abuse both physic and surgery."

*An Elizabethan quack offers a patient the quick remedy of one of his concoctions.*

people had no way of knowing that skin that looked clean could really be dirty. Instead, both men and women handled the problem of odor with liberal use of perfumes and colognes. One of the strongest perfume bases was made of musk from the anal pouch of a civet, a large cat found in Asia and Africa. The civet's musk was so popular, in fact, that perfume sellers used an image of the animal as their emblem.

Another means of keeping odors at bay was the use of pomanders, which were little bags of scented herbs and flowers that could be hung in various places throughout the house. They were put between bed sheets, around the bed curtains, and in drawers. Queen Elizabeth, who was said to be very sensitive to odors, had a number of pomanders dangling from the roof of her carriage so she did not have to be bothered by the odor of the city when she traveled. She, like many women of the upper and middle classes, had necklaces that were pomanders, containing a paste of perfume.

## Fox Grease and Dead Mice

The lack of personal hygiene and the presence of hazards in water, in the home, and in poorly stored foods, lead to many health problems in Elizabethan London. Coughs, colds, fevers, and intestinal woes such as dysentery and food poisoning were common ailments. But the medical knowledge of the sixteenth century was a cross between knowledge and superstition, and cures made patients sicker as often as they relieved their symptoms.

For example, poor eyesight was believed to be caused by someone looking at fire, smoke, and Greek books—and by eating onions and garlic. To restore eyesight, wrote one physician during the mid-1500s, it was important to look at things that were healthy for eyes. "Everything that is green or black is good for a man to look upon it," he wrote. "Also to look upon gold is good for the sight, and so is glass, cold water, and every cold thing."[75]

Some of the remedies involved substances that were difficult to obtain. Grease from a fox, for example, was supposed to be able to cure baldness. The gout could be cured by "cutting a mouse in twain and lay it to the legs."[76] Physicians were usually strong believers in the influence of the stars and the planets on health and in the healing powers of amulets, charms, and even a king's or queen's touch.

## The Surgeon

It was the physician who diagnosed the problem, and when the likely cause of the disease or illness was detected, a surgeon was called upon. Viewed more as craftsmen, surgeons were not as esteemed as physicians. Nonetheless, they were responsible for performing operations deemed necessary to restore a patient to health. Surgeons used a variety of treatments, many of which seem brutal by modern standards. Writes one historian,

> They pulled out teeth with tongs, straightened fractures by sheer physical strength, and amputated legs

and arms, in all cases without any kind of anaesthetic, while the patient was given a good dose of alcohol and was held down by surgeon's assistants . . . [and] wounds were cauterized by applying a burning iron or boiling oil to the wound.[77]

Bloodletting, though, was a surgeon's most common method for fighting illness. Illness was thought to be the result of too much blood, or of evil blood. By removing evil from the blood, physicians believed, a patient was more apt to receive God's grace and avoid wickedness that could cause disease. To remove bad blood, surgeons either cut a vein with an instrument called a lancet, or applied leeches on the skin to suck out the blood.

## Smallpox and the Sweat

In addition to common ailments and injuries, physicians and surgeons had to grapple with some very frightening diseases during Elizabeth's reign. Two much-feared diseases were smallpox and something called "the sweat." Smallpox was a relative newcomer on the medical scene; it first appeared in England in 1514. There was no cure for the disease, whose symptoms were a high fever and rash. Queen Elizabeth herself almost died from smallpox; she was comatose and the court physician pronounced her very close to death. However, her high fever lessened several hours later and she survived, although it is believed that she

went bald shortly afterward—a common side effect of battling the disease.

Elizabethan physicians had no idea how to treat smallpox victims, but they tried many drastic and unusual remedies. One was to place the patient in a meat-pickling container and fumigate him with cinnabar, a chemical containing mercury. "After [that] he must be given a drastic sweating treatment," explains one historian, "and kept on a low diet. There is then perhaps a chance left that he may recover."[78]

Equally mystifying was a disease known as the sweat, which was frightening mostly because of its suddenness and severity. People who felt quite well could be struck as they were eating a meal or lying in their beds. They would become drenched in sweat and have difficulty breathing. Within several hours, they might be dead. As one man of the day observed, "Some merry at dinner, and dead at supper."[79] On the other hand, if someone could survive the first eighteen to twenty-four hours, it was likely that he or she would live.

The sweat is believed to have first occurred in England during the late fifteenth century, and outbreaks occurred nine or ten times during the sixteenth and early seventeenth centuries. Scientists today are not certain what the sweat was or how it was contracted.

## Two Types of Plague

Smallpox and the sweat claimed thousands of people during the Elizabethan era, but no disease was more feared than the bubonic plague and its close relative, the pneumonic plague. Both types struck Europe during the fourteenth century, and several severe outbreaks occurred in England up through the seventeenth century.

Plague was, in Elizabeth's time, a disease of the towns and cities; farmers and other country dwellers were far less likely to catch it. When it occurred in London, it did a great deal of damage, sometimes killing 25 to 30 percent of the city's population. By far the worst outbreaks in London occurred in 1563, in 1578 through 1579, in 1592, and in 1603.

The outbreaks were frustratingly random: One town might be infected during one year, but another town might see no cases of the plague. It was also common to see both types of plague, pneumonic and bubonic, during an outbreak. One of the few things that physicians of the day understood was that summer was usually the time when the plague struck hardest, and as with many illnesses, children and old people were most at risk.

The cause of either type of plague was a mystery to the Elizabethans. It is understood today that the bubonic plague originated with a particular type of flea that lived on the backs of certain black rats. That is what made crowded cities and towns so vulnerable to that variety of plague. As one historian explains, many Elizabethan houses, "with a wooden framework filled in with clay and plaster, a refuse-heap before the door, and filthy rushes upon the floor, provided the black rat with an ideal home."[80]

*Victims of the plague are dumped from a cart into a mass grave.*

A rat with the disease would die— usually inside a home—and the fleas living on it, which were also infected, would jump to a human as a source of blood and warmth. A single flea bite infected a human with the plague. First, the victim might notice that a flea bite was changing colors, usually red to purplish black. Then, his or her lymph nodes under the arms and on the sides of the neck would become sore and enlarged. The victim would begin running a high fever, up to 106 degrees. With the fever would come chills, aching limbs, confusion, delerium, and, usually in three or four days, death. A person who became infected had only a 30 to 40 percent chance of survival.

When the plague infected a person's lungs, it could become a far more virulent strain, called pneumonic plague. Unlike bubonic plague, which was not contagious from person to person (only from rat to flea to human) the pneumonic plague was quickly spread in tiny droplets of a sneeze or a cough from one person to another. The mortality rate was virtually 100 percent.

## "The Purple Whip of Vengeance"

Since knowledge of germs and disease was almost nonexistent during the sixteenth century, people viewed the plague as a virtual death sentence that could be explained only by some supernatural power. Some thought it had to do with evil poisons in the air, and others believed it was caused by some unfortunate alignment among the planets.

Perhaps the most common belief, however, was that the plague was God's way of punishing people for wickedness; it was sometimes known as "the purple whip of vengeance."[81] So deeply was this belief felt, in fact, that members of the clergy insisted that fighting the disease with anything other than prayer was immoral and sinful since the plague was an instrument of God.

## Preventing Certain Death

Although there was neither a cure nor an idea of how to prevent the plague, people were willing to try a variety of remedies suggested by various physicians and chemists of the day, including burning old shoes and inhaling the smoke, placing a red-hot brick in a vat of vinegar, and applying special pomanders of oranges and cloves. At least one London physician advised a patient to drink a mixture of wine, salad oil, and gunpowder. Several experts maintained that leaving four or five peeled onions on the ground for ten days would attract and absorb all of the infection in that area of the city.

However, as the death toll mounted and nothing seemed to work, it became more clear that since there were no remedies for the plague, people should spend their energy preventing infection. The wisest way seemed to be avoiding contact with plague victims; although they had no concept of germs, the fact that whole families were sick made it obvious that the disease spread somehow.

## "Cast Out Your Dead"

To protect themselves, the citizens of London organized a method of keeping sick people (and those who were in danger of catching the plague from them) away from others. During the outbreak of 1563, any house whose inhabitants had the plague was required by law to have posted on it a blue cross on white paper with the words "Lord have mercy upon us" written on it.

# "Like Mourners at Some Great Solemn Funeral"

*One of the most vivid descriptions of the fear inspired by the plague in Elizabethan times was written by an English playwright named Thomas Dekker, who published this account in 1609. This excerpt is included in* The Tudor Age, *by A.F. Scott.*

The purple whip of vengeance, the plague, having beaten many thousands of men, women, and children to death, and still marking the people of this city every week by hundreds for the grave, is the only cause that all her inhabitants walk up and down like mourners at some great solemn funeral, the City herself being the chief mourners. The poison of this lingering infection strikes so deep into all men's hearts that their cheeks, like cowardly soldiers, have lost their colours; theire eyes, as if they were in debt and durst [dare] not long abroad, do scarce peep out of their heads; and their tongues, like physicians ill paid, give but cold comfort.

By the power of their pestilent charms all merry meetings are cut off, all frolic assemblies dissolved, and in their circles are raised up the black, sullen, and dogged spirits of sadness, of melancholy, and so, consequently, of mischief. Mirth [happiness] is departed and lies dead and buried in men's bosoms; laughter dares not look a man in the face; jests are, like music to the deaf, not regarded; leisure itself finds now no pleasure but in sighing and bewailing the miseries of the time. For, alack! What string is there now to be played upon whose touch can make us merry? Playhouses stand like taverns that have cast out their masters, the doors locked up, the flags . . . taken down—or rather like houses lately infected, from whence the affrighted dwellers are fled, in hope to live better in the country.

The windows and doors of the house were to remain closed for forty days, and official watchmen ensured that no one, not even healthy family members, left the premises. When the door did open, it usually meant that the patient had died and the body was being taken outside for the corpse bearer. He made his way through the city each day pushing a large cart, ringing his bell, and calling "Cast out your dead!" or "Have you any dead bodies to bury?"

Although the bearers were performing an important function, many citizens disliked them for what seemed like a callous, indifferent attitude toward the victims. One witness wrote in 1563 that corpse bearers were a crew of nasty men who "did affright [scare] the people most sadly by their swearing and cursing."[82]

## The Pest Pit

Ordinances also dealt with the way the dead were buried. To limit public exposure to the infected corpses, the city limited the number of mourners who could accompany the body to the grave site to six, not including the minister and bearer. City officials also made it illegal to hold a burial when people were apt to be on the streets; no one could be buried before 10:00 P.M.

During the plague of 1603, more than thirty-eight thousand Londoners died—too many for London's graveyards to hold. It was difficult to find a coffin, and if a family could locate one for a funeral, it was extremely expensive. The answer to both problems was the pest pit. A corpse was wrapped in a long sheet and was flung into this mass grave, usually along with forty or more other corpses. One Londoner described, with gruesome detail, a visit to such a pest pit:

> Lord! what a sight was there? and
>   what strong smells
> Ascended from among Death's
>   loathsome Cells? . . .
> Yonn lay a heape of skulls; another
>   there;
> Here, halfe unburied did a Corpse
>   appeare . . .
> A locke of woman's hayre; a dead
>   man's face
> Uncover'd; and a ghastly sight it was.[83]

## Shutting Down the City

During outbreaks, there was fear not only of those who already were sick but also of those seemingly healthy people who might soon be infected. At these times, public gatherings other than church ser-

*A contemporary woodcut depicts Londoners fleeing an outbreak of plague. A pair of skeletons, allegorical figures of death, hovers menacingly over the fugitives.*

vices were banned. Sporting events, plays, and other activities that normally drew crowds were discontinued.

There were other regulations, too. Beggars were banned from church, with the idea that they were more likely to be struck with the disease. Travelers were urged to stay away from the city. Londoners themselves left the city, hoping they could sidestep death by visiting relatives in the country or a small town. One sixteenth-century writer describes hordes of people fleeing "in wagons, carts, and horses, full laden with young bairns [children], for fear of the Black Pestilence, with their boxes of medicines and sweet perfumes."[84] But many country people were suspicious of these refugees, and believing the city folk to be carrying disease, often drove them away violently.

The plague years were terrifying times for the city's inhabitants. Many agreed with Thomas Dekker, a playwright and essayist of the era, who used what he believed to be a fitting plea for mercy in ghastly times: "Lord, have mercy upon London."

# Crime in Elizabethan London

**B**esides the fear of death by the plague, there was nothing that threatened the order of Elizabethan life as much as crime. It was common, however, especially in London. Citizens were victims of a wide variety of crimes, ranging from petty theft to murder.

Criminals came from all classes, but a great deal of London's crime originated in some of the poorest areas, where people without employment—or hope for employment—idled. Within these areas of the city there was a growing class of people called *rogues* and *vagabonds* who were usually up to no good. Much of the city's crime originated with them.

## A Threat to the Traveler

Anyone traveling to or from London was in danger from some of these rogues. Even the best roads were in bad shape; most were narrow and often enclosed on both sides by overgrowth. These were, unfortunately, easy places for a robber—known as a highwayman—to lie in wait with a dagger in his hand.

Not all of these men were seasoned criminals. Some were young men who had gambled away their money or who lived far beyond their means. Some were soldiers, discharged from duty, with no idea of what to do next. And some, explains one writer of the time, "were servingmen [servants] whose wages cannot suffice so much as to find them breeches."[86]

76

Highwaymen were usually certain that the travelers they attacked had a lot of money. One Elizabethan traveler insists that the highwaymen were usually tipped off by a dishonest innkeeper where a traveler had spent the night, probably for a percentage of the victim's money: "I believe that not . . . a traveller in England is robbed by the way without the knowledge of some of them [innkeepers], for when he cometh into the inn, and alighteth from his horse, the hostler forthwith is very busy to take down his budget [leather bag of money] . . . which he [weighs] slyly in his hand to feel the weight thereof."[87]

## "Some Desperate Cutters We Have"

If a traveler to London thought his worries would be over after reaching the city, he was sadly mistaken. The streets, especially those in the poorer sections of town, were risky even during the daylight hours, and the citizens knew it. One was naive, writes one observer of the day, if he thought he did not need to be armed to protect himself:

Our nobility wear commonly swords . . . with their daggers, as doth every common servingman also that followeth his lord and master. Some desperate cutters [swordsmen] we have in like sort, which carry two daggers or two rapiers [double-edged swords] in a sheath always about them, wherewith in every drunken fray they are known to work much mischief.[88]

Petty thieves also abounded. Pickpockets were experts in relieving passersby of their purses or watches without their knowledge. It was almost impossible to catch a pickpocket, for such a thief was said to have had the three attributes a surgeon should have: an eagle eye, a lion's heart, and a woman's hand "to be lithe and nimble," wrote one man in 1591, "and better

*A highwayman robs a nobleman's carriage. The country roads to London were fraught with danger.*

to dive into the pocket."[89] The cutpurse, another form of thief, was outfitted with a little knife that he wore on his fingers; when he brushed up against a pedestrian, he would slice the leather strap of a bag or purse and disappear into the crowd with his loot.

## The Men on the Beat

With a number of crimes being committed daily in the city, one might suspect that the Elizabethans were not concerned with crime or that they had no laws to protect their citizens. Not so, say historians; if anything, the Elizabethans were eager to punish wrongdoers and to punish them severe-

ly. Writes L.F. Salzman, "If the people were brutal, the law was ferocious."[90]

This was an age when the death penalty was freely applied. The Elizabethans used it not just for murders and treason but also for the theft of more than two shillings. In England about one thousand criminals each year were executed in a number of ways, most of them public. The problem was not the lack of law but rather the difficulty of its enforcement.

Although red-coated constables walked the streets of the neighborhoods night and day, they prevented few crimes. Citizens complained that they were often drunk on duty and were often so old and

## The Ducking Stool

*A punishment almost always reserved for women accused of prostitution, scolding, or other disturbances of the peace was the ducking stool, a simple machine set up at a nearby pond. In his book* Old-Time Punishments, *William Andrews gives a detailed description of it.*

It [the ducking stool] consists merely of a strong narrow under framework, placed on four wheels, of solid wood, about four inches in thickness, and eighteen in diameter. At one end of the framework two upright posts, about three feet in height, strongly embedded in the platform, carry a long movable beam. Each of the arms of this beam are of equal length (13 feet), and balance perfectly from the top of the post. The culprit placed in the seat naturally weighs down that one end into the water, while the other is lifted up in the air; men, however, with ropes, caused the uplifted end to rise or fall, and thus obtain a perfect see-saw. The purchase of the machine is such that the culprit can be launched forth some 16 to 18 feet into the pond or stream, while the administrators of the ducking stand on dry land.

heavy that they were incapable of chasing down even the slowest thief. One of the most frequent complaints, however, was that the constables were often indifferent when a citizen reported a crime. Says William Harrison, "Sometimes constables, when summoned to pursue thieves, would say: 'God restore your loss! I have other business at this time.'"[91]

## Courts and the Neck Verse

Occasionally, however, a constable did apprehend a criminal and bring him before a city judge. There were various courts in London, depending on the person's social rank and also the nature of the crime. Petty theft, for example, might be heard by a judge in one court, but a more serious crime, such as murder or large-scale theft, would be handled in another. Certain cases, such as adultery, drunkenness, or failing to baptize one's child, were heard by a church court run by the archdeacon of a parish.

Back in the Middle Ages, a tradition began that continued into Elizabethan times. If the accused criminal was a priest, he would receive a much more lenient sentence than a layperson. The way a criminal could prove he was a priest was to read a passage from the Bible aloud and in Latin to the judge, because during the Middle Ages only clergy could read and write. An accused criminal attempting to do so was considered to be "pleading the benefit of clergy."

The verse used most often was part of the fifty-first Psalm, which was known as the neck verse since successfully reading it would save a man from hanging. After Catholicism was banned from England, the law still remained on the books, a loophole that allowed a criminal to dodge a death sentence merely by demonstrating his ability to read. By the early 1800s, however, the loophole was finally eliminated since so many citizens could read and write.

## Torture at the Tower of London

Most criminals could not plead the benefit of clergy, though, and were doomed to be punished in one of many ways. Punishments varied according to the severity of the crime. The harshest punishments were reserved for those who committed acts of treason. This was the most serious crime in Elizabethan times, for it usually involved a plot against the throne.

The ordeal that awaited one convicted of treason was unimaginably agonizing. The prisoner was usually taken to the Tower of London—an infamous high-security prison that was the site of unspeakable acts of torture on political criminals—usually in order to elicit confessions or gain information about their coconspirators. The instrument most often used at the Tower of London was the rack, which could produce excruciating pain. One historian describes the rack:

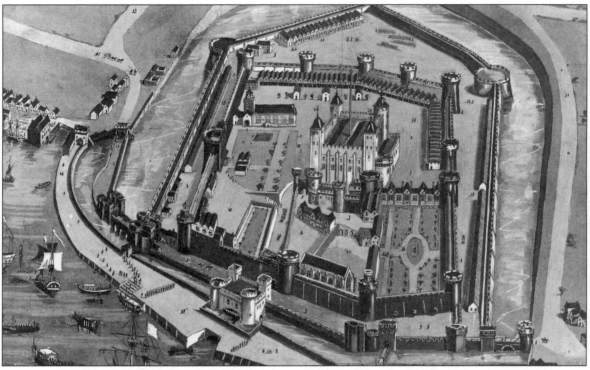

*An engraving portrays the appearance of the Tower of London during the Elizabethan age. Criminals convicted of treason were subjected to excruciating acts of torture in the Tower.*

[It] was a horizontal frame within which the prisoner was placed, with ropes attached to his wrists and ankles. The ropes were wound around cylindrical rollers at each end of the frame. When the rollers were turned, the prisoner might eventually be pulled apart at his joints. . . . The rack's advantage was that the pain could be applied gradually, allowing the victim to sense what was coming.[92]

## The Death Penalty

Occasionally a prisoner on the rack died from the agony of being pulled apart; however, once guards got the information they were looking for, they released him into his cell. There, he would await whatever death sentence the court had decided on. Some traitors were beheaded—not by a sharp-bladed guillotine but by two or three whacks of the executioner's axe. A few hardened criminals during Elizabeth's reign were boiled to death, a practice that began during the early 1500s by Elizabeth's father, Henry VIII. But by far, the most common death penalty was the three-step method: being hanged, drawn, and finally quartered.

This, like all death sentences, was carried out in a public square to make an example of the wrongdoer. The Elizabethans hoped that this would deter others from committing similar crimes. The accused was taken to the gallows and then, according to the sentence read aloud preceding the execution, hanged by the neck "until he be half dead, and then cut down; and his entrails to be cut out of his body and burnt by the executioner; then his head is to be cut off, his body to be divided into quarters to be set up in some open place directed."[93] Almost always, the criminal's head was impaled on a long pike and set on London Bridge to serve as a reminder of what would happen to such traitors.

## Amputations and Brands

Less serious crimes were punished by administering intense physical pain, too. Jails and prisons were rarely used to hold criminals for years, as they are in modern times. The Elizabethans had neither the space nor the money to maintain felons in prison. Instead, punishments tended to be short and harsh.

For example, thieves—even those who had stolen the equivalent of a few dollars—were often sentenced to have some part of their body amputated. Occasionally, a hand or a thumb was lopped off, but most judges preferred an amputation that was less severe, such as an ear or earlobe. That way, the amputation would not keep a criminal from doing physical work after his punishment was finished.

In addition, many were branded with a red-hot iron in the shape of a meaning-ful letter. A brand in the shape of a **T** was used if the accused was a thief, or a **D** if he was a drunkard. This sort of permanent disfigurement served two purposes: It was painful, and it prevented the wrongdoer from claiming in the future to be a first-time offender.

## Pillories and Stocks

Another common punishment for a less-dangerous criminal was a specified time in

*A criminal is stretched on the rack to extract a confession of guilt.*

either the pillory or the stocks. Both were set up in public areas, such as a marketplace, and were meant to be both uncomfortable and humiliating. The pillory was a wooden stand with oversized semicircles cut into it to restrain a person's head and arms. Standing at the pillory, even for a few hours, was hard on the back, and the humiliation of having passersby taunt and throw eggs or even hit the criminal while restrained made the time in the pillory even worse. Occasionally the punishment could be made more severe by authorizing the constable or guard to nail the criminal's ear to the pillory.

Often the pillory was used as punishment for the crime of trickery, such as a grocer or baker selling a container that appeared to be full but was really not. In 1552, for example, a man in the Cheapside district of London was pilloried for selling pots of strawberries that were not even half full; instead, they were mostly filled with ferns.

Stocks, too, were restrictive, much like an open-air jail. They were similar to the pillory, except they held the criminal's legs instead of his arms and head. Stocks were used for punishing habitual brawlers, vagrants, and drunks. The time spent restrained in stocks could be anywhere from a few hours to an entire day and night. In 1584, say historians, three men caught stealing wood "were set in the stocks two days, in the open street, with the stolen wood before them, as a punishment."[94]

# Crimes and Punishments

*The Elizabethans kept track of criminals' records and what punishment was assigned for each offense. Below are several entries in the Essex Record Office from the late sixteenth century. These are included in A.F. Scott's* The Tudor Age.

—Thomas Botesworth is fined . . . because he is a common brawler and disturber of his neighbors and to give him warning to leave it or else he is to be carried in a dung cart about the town in an open assembly, and then to be put in the stocks and then to be banished out of the lordship.

—The wife of Walter Hycocks and the wife of Peter Philips do be common scolds and therefore it is ordered that they shall be admonished thereof in the church, to leave their scolding. But upon complaint made by their neighbors the second time they shall be punished by the ducking stool according to the direction of the constable.

—Agnes Osier alias Beggar of Brok Street in South Weald, Spinster, for breaking into the house of William Reynolds of the same in the night-time, and stealing two flaxen sheets . . . belonging to the said William. Guilty: to be hanged.

# The Scold's Bridle

Women were not exempt from physical or humiliating punishments; in fact, one of the most painful and demeaning punishments was reserved for women. It was known as the scold's bridle, a contraption worn as a punishment for a woman who spoke loudly or angrily in public, especially to her husband.

The bridle was made of iron and was shaped very much like a birdcage. It had four or six bars extending down from the top. There was an iron plate in front, which was either very sharp or was covered with spikes. According to expert William Andrews, the plate was "so situated as to be placed in the mouth of the victim, and if she attempted to move her tongue in any way whatever, it was certain to be shockingly injured."[95]

After the constable placed the bridle on the woman's head, he lead her through the town, holding a chain that was attached to the bridle. Some of the bridles also had bells to further call attention to the women wearing them. Occasionally the bridle was used at home, too; a husband could send for the constable, urging him to bring the bridle. After bridling the wife, the constable chained the strap to the hook on the fireplace, says Andrews, "until she promised to behave herself better for the future."[96]

# Witches

Witchcraft was another crime for which women were sometimes accused. During Elizabethan times almost all people

*An illustration depicts an Elizabethan witch in a high-crowned, pointed hat.*

believed in the existence of witches. No matter what one's social rank, level of schooling, or religious training, witches were considered a terrifying threat to the well-being of citizens. A noted lawyer of the day defined a witch as "a person who hath conference with the Devil, to consult with him or to do some act."[97] And a German duke, visiting in 1592, noted that "many witches are found there, who frequently do much mischief by means of hail and tempests."[98]

On the European continent, witches were reported flying through the air on broomsticks and joining with other witches

# Testing for a Witch

*Elizabethans used several methods to test whether a woman accused of witchcraft really was a witch. The following is one method that was suggested to an officer of the court by a man experienced in witch testing. Written during the early seventeenth century, the account is included in R.E. Pritchard's* Shakespeare's England.

His friend understanding this, advised him to take them [the accused women], or any one of them, to his mill dam, having first shut up the mill gates that the water might be at highest, and then, binding their arms across, stripping them into their smocks, and leaving their legs at liberty, throw them into the water. Yet lest they should not be witches and that their lives might not be in danger of drowning, let their be a rope tied about their middles, so long as it may reach from one side of your dam to the other, where on each side let one of your men stand, that if she chance to sink they may draw her up and preserve her. Then if she swim, take her up . . . I have seen it often tried in the north country. . . .

At which his men presently recovered, bound her to their master's horse, and brought her home . . . and did as before the gentleman had advised him; when, being thrown in . . . she sank some two feet in the water with a fall, but rose again, and floated upon the water like a plank.

*A woman accused of witchcraft is dunked in water to determine the validity of the allegation.*

in covens, but the witches in sixteenth-century England were somewhat tamer. According to one expert, English witches were mostly accused of "killing their neighbor's cows, deforming children's toes, and causing trees to fall on barns."[99] The allegations against certain women were often made by families who had come into bad luck. Blaming a poor crop, a child's death, or a failing business on witchcraft was easier than trying to explain it another way. One man who accused a woman of witchery in 1584 alleged that the woman was responsible for bad things happening to him, all because he had refused to give her some milk: "She [the accused] was at my house of late, she would have had a pot of milk. She departed in a [rage] because she had it not. She railed, she cursed, she mumbled and whispered, and finally she said she would be even with me. And soon after, my child, my sow, or my pullet [hen] died, or was strangely taken."[100]

## Punishing Witches

Sometimes a witch was brought before a church courts, where an official ordered them to bring in several neighbors who could swear to her good character. If she could do that, she would be released. If, however, any of the neighbors doubted her, she would be given some sort of public punishment, such as appearing in church wearing a long white sheet wrapped around her body. She would be ordered to beg the forgiveness of the townspeople and God for her evil ways. If a woman was tried in a city court, the punishment was much more severe. A woman who maintained her innocence and refused to repent, even when others swore she was guilty, might be hanged or burned at the stake.

Occasionally a judge who was not convinced of a woman's guilt would utilize one of the era's standard methods for proving innocence or guilt. One method, known as the swimming test, involved tying the woman's right thumb to her left big toe and throwing her into a deep pond. "Suspects who floated," explains one historian, "were thought to have been aided by the Devil, and their guilt was assumed. Suspects who did not float were fished out and attempts were made, not always successfully, to revive them."[101]

Women accused of witchcraft, like other accused criminals of Elizabethan times, were rarely given the benefit of the doubt. Just as thousands of criminals were never apprehended, there were no doubt thousands of people punished or executed for crimes they did not commit. But crime upset the harmony and balance of life; if their law specifying punishments seemed brutal or harsh, to the Elizabethans it was simply a necessary brutality.

# Chapter 8

# Pleasure and Sport

Life may have been brief and diffi-cult during the Elizabethan era, but people still knew how to enjoy themselves. One traveler noted that people in England, more than in any other nation, were obsessed with all sorts of pleasure:

> All Cities, Towns, and villages swarm with companies of musicians and fiddlers, which are rare in other kingdoms. The City of London alone hath four or five companies of players with their particular theaters capable of many thousands, wherein they all play every day in the week but Sunday. . . . Not to speak of frequent spectacles in London exhibited to the people by fencers, by walkers on ropes, and like men of activity, nor of frequent companies of archers shooting in all the fields.[102]

## Music Everywhere

Music was an enormous part of everyday life during the 1500s. People took pleasure in creating music rather than merely listening to it. Almost every home had at least one instrument, usually a stringed instrument such as a six-stringed viol or a lute. Lutes were so common that barbers put them in their shops as modern barbers lay out magazines.

Rounds and madrigals, songs written for four- or five-part harmony, were often sung at home after dinner, no matter what the family's social class. The after-dinner singing time was highly anticipated, especially if guests were present who might have a new song to teach. One Elizabethan man recalled in 1597 that for a guest to refrain from singing was considered very rude: "Supper being ended and the Music books, according to the custom, being brought to the table: the mistress of the house presented me with a part, earnestly requesting me to sing. But when after many excuses, I protested that I could not, everyone began to wonder. Yea, some whispered to others, demanding how I was brought up."[103]

## "What Filthie Groping"

Dancing was also a popular activity among all classes, although the types of dances preferred by the wealthy classes differed significantly from those favored by the common people. Nobles prided themselves on learning dances that involved complex steps and usually involved only two dancers. Common people enjoyed the folk dances of England as well as new dances from places such as France and Scotland.

Regardless of class, people danced at parties and gatherings during holidays; in

*An Elizabethan woman sings to the accompaniment of her lover playing the lute. Making music was a common diversion in sixteenth-century England.*

the country dances also were held at harvest time. Few people, young or old, wanted to miss a dance. It was a pleasant way to interact with others; the queen herself is said to have enjoyed dancing more than almost any other physical activity. One rumor circulating in 1593 was that she danced a complicated French dance with a visiting French duke "who was so delighted with her performance that he artfully made shift to kiss not her hand but also her foot."[104]

But as popular as dancing was, many conservative English church officials disapproved. There was too much touching and too many opportunities for wrongdoing, warned moralist Phillip Stubbes in 1583. "What clipping and culling, what kissing and bussing," he asked, "what smooching and slavering one of another,

# A Letter Against Stage Play

*Many conservatives of the day, especially clergymen, objected to what they considered a dangerous development, namely, the theaters in London. In 1597 the lord mayor of the city, as well as the aldermen (councilmen), wrote a letter to the city's legislature hoping that stage plays could be banned. This excerpt from the letter is contained in Leonard Ashley's* Elizabethan Popular Culture.

Our humble duties remembered to your good Lords and the rest. We have signified to your Honors many times heretofore the great inconvenience which we find to grow by the common exercise of stage-plays. We presume to do [so], as well in respect of the duty we bear towards her Highness for the good government of this her city, as for conscience sake, being persuaded (under correction of your Honors' judgment) that neither in polity [government] nor in religion they are to be suffered [allowed] in a Christian commonwealth, specially being of that frame and matter as usually they are, containing nothing but profane fables, lascivious [lewd] matters, cozening [fraudulent] devices, and scurrilous [coarse] behaviors, which are so set forth as that they move wholly to imitation and not to the avoiding of those faults and vices which they represent. Among other inconveniences it is not the least that they give opportunity to the refuse [garbage] sort of evil-disposed and ungodly people that are within and about this city to assemble themselves and to make their matches for all their lewd and ungodly practices.

what filthie groping and uncleane handling is not practised in those dancings?"[105]

## The Theater

One activity that has become synonymous with Elizabethan times is the theater. People loved going to plays, and during the late sixteenth century nowhere on Earth offered more choices of plays than London. Most of the theaters were built just outside the city limits, south of the Thames. That way, they were outside the legal jurisdiction of city officials who might find reason to arrest some of the poorer playgoers for vagrancy or to close a theater for some violation, such as having seating that was unsafe.

The works of brilliant dramatists were put on by these theaters. Christopher Marlowe was a popular playwright; his play *Tamburlaine the Great* was a tremendous success, for it had a huge cast and an exciting plot. Marlowe was said to have influenced the greatest Elizabethan playwright of them all, William Shakespeare. Shakespeare began writing plays during the early 1590s and was Elizabeth's favorite.

The Elizabethans were not refined theatergoers. They were not interested in subtle plots. They wanted loud, exciting speeches and plenty of action. Battle scenes, especially, were great favorites of the crowd. Knowing how patrons loved gore in drama, the theater owners would get blood and sheep guts from local butchers and use them as props for sword fights.

## A Penny Per Ticket

A few indoor theaters existed in London, but by far the busiest ones were open-air theaters. These theaters were circular in shape, with galleries around the sides. Plays were perfomed in daylight, for there was no aritificial lighting in those days, nor was there scenery or musical background. The costumes, on the other hand, were amazing. One sixteenth-century writer explained how actors acquired the colorful, rich wardrobe they used on stage: "The play-actors are dressed most exquisitely and elegantly, because of the custom in England that when men of rank or knights die they give and bequeath almost their finest apparel to their servants, who, since it does not befit them, do not wear such garments, but afterwards let the play-actors buy them for a few pence."[106]

Those who came to watch the plays were from every social class, and at many performances the theaters—some with a capacity of three thousand—were filled. Admission was usually a penny (a lot of money in those days), so poorer people could not afford to attend too often. Those who wanted some refreshment could summon one of the young men wandering through the crowd during the performance selling apples, pears, nuts, and beer.

## Blood Sports

Theaters competed for customers with the men who ran the bullbaiting and bearbaiting amusements. These were

*A scene from a contemporary production of Shakespeare's* Hamlet. *Theatergoing was one of the most popular forms of entertainment in Elizabethan London.*

held on Sundays in London, in arenas much like open-air theaters, with wooden galleries set up for spectators. More than one thousand people crowded into the arena. Most paid a penny for admission. Two pennies guaranteed a spectator a good seat in the galleries.

The baiting event began when a collared bull or bear was brought in and chained so that its movement was limited. The "baiting" was done by dogs, which, upon a signal from their owner, set at the animal, growling and attacking it from all sides. One first-time visitor to a bearbaiting described the experience:

It was a sport very pleasant . . . to see the bear with his pink eyes leering after his enemies' approach, the nimbleness and wait of the dog to take his advantage, and the force and experience of the bear again to avoid the assaults . . . with biting, with clawing, with roaring, tossing and tumbling he would work to wind himself from them: and when he was loose to shake his ears twice or thrice with the blood and the slaver [saliva] about his physiognomy.[107]

At least a few of the dogs were killed during the baiting, and others were injured

# Smoking and Bear Whipping

*In his visit to England, the German traveler Paul Hentzner described what he found to be an exciting end to a bearbaiting. In this excerpt from his essay, which is included in A.F. Scott's* The Tudor Age, *Hentzner found his attention torn between the whipping of the bear and the use of tobacco by the crowd.*

To this entertainment there often follows that of whipping a blinded bear, which is performed by five or six men, standing in a circle with whips, which they exercise upon him without any mercy. Although he cannot escape from them because of his chain, he nevertheless defends himself, vigorously throwing down all who come within his reach and are not active enough to get out of it, and tearing the whips out of their hands and breaking them.

At these spectacles and everywhere else, the English are constantly smoking the Nicotian weed which in America is called *Tobaca*—all others call it *Paetum*—and generally in this manner: they have pipes on purpose made of clay, into the farther end of which they put the herb, so dry that it may be rubbed into powder, and lighting it, they draw the smoke into their mouths, which they puff out again through their nostrils, like funnels, along with it plenty of phlegm and defluxion [discharge] from the head.

*Bearbaiting drew large crowds of Elizabethans. Here, a bear beset by dogs breaks its chain and threatens spectators.*

or too frightened to continue. The owner usually had one hundred or more dogs on hand, just in case. When necessary, a new batch of dogs was thrown into the arena to continue the attack.

Historians say that baiting was an amusement that was enjoyed by people of all social classes, not just the commoners. The spectators enjoyed the blood and gore, and they placed bets with one another on the outcome. Even Elizabeth enjoyed it; she occasionally had bearbaiting at the royal palace for an evening's entertainment.

## Rough Sports

There were equally violent sports that people played themselves rather than merely watched. Wrestling matches were popular, and there were few rules. It was common for ribs to be crushed during a wrestling match in the city, and country wrestling matches were known to be even rougher and bloodier.

Cudgel play, another violent sport, involved two players trying to hit one another with wooden clubs. The object was to draw blood from one's opponent's skull. "A red streak pouring from the scalp down

*Elizabethan athletes play the tame sport of tennis, which had been invented in the thirteenth century.*

the face," explains one expert, "signified the loser—conscious or unconscious. The winner might, happily, escape with a broken arm or dislocated shoulder."[108]

But the roughest contest by far was soccer, or football, as the Elizabethans knew it. The game was not new during Elizabethan times; it had existed in some form since the ancient Greeks and Romans. Some who admired the game, such as esteemed schoolmaster Richard Mulcaster, were convinced that it had possibilities. Mulcaster often stated that if a few rules were added and young men could be persuaded to take the time to learn the subtleties of the game and to play it within those rules, it could be a positive experience, teaching them teamwork and promoting health.

## "Sometimes Their Necks Are Broken"

However, even Mulcaster saw that the Elizabethans were not interested in learning the complexities of the game, nor were they willing to try adding new rules. Their style of soccer was not healthy in the least, as he complained in 1581: "As it is now commonly used . . . with bursting of shins and breaking of legs, it be neither civil, neither worthy the name of any train to health."[109]

Another observer agreed with Mulcaster, calling soccer little more than "a friendly kind of fight . . . a bloody and murdering practice," and tried to explain in detail what he had seen at a recent soccer match in London:

Sometimes their necks are broken, sometimes their backs, sometimes their legs, sometimes their arms; sometime one part thrust out of joint, sometime another; sometimes the noses gush with blood, sometimes their eyes start out. . . . But whoseoever scapeth away the best goeth not scot free, but is either sore wounded, crazed and bruised, so that he dieth of it, or else scapeth very hardly.[110]

The passions on the soccer field also led to dangerous fights afterward, often involving exhuberant spectators. At university matches, for example, both students and fans occasionally arrived on the field with weapons, just in case a brawl erupted afterward. One man wrote about a crowd of spectators looking for a fight who "did pick quarrels against one [university] team and did bring out" clubs, which they had hidden before the match, and beat the players so hard that several "had their heads broken."[111] Elizabeth issued an order in 1561 banning soccer matches for being too dangerous, but they continued anyway.

## Hoodman Blind and Hot Cockles

Girls almost never participated in sports like cudgel play and soccer, but there were some games that both boys and girls played. One, called hoodman blind, was similar to the modern children's game blindman's buff. A player, blinded by a cloth hood over his or her head, tried to catch other players, who slapped or cuffed the "hoodman." If the hoodman caught one of the others and was able to guess his or her identity, they could trade places. If not, the hoodman was doomed to continue wearing the hood.

Another game, hot cockles, was often played at Christmas festivities. This game involved one player leaning over into another's lap while being slapped on the rear end by the others. The object was the same as in hoodman blind—to guess the identity of the last person to slap him.

Of course, there were many games played by the Elizabethans that did not involve slapping or other horseplay. Many people enjoyed playing chess, dice, and a game called Irish, which was almost identical to backgammon. Yet few people played games simply for the competition or fun; for most Elizabethans, games, whether cards or a footrace, were of little interest unless they could wager on the outcome. Even children wagered on any game, using cherry stones they kept in their pockets.

*A group of children plays blindman's buff in this 1932 photo. The modern amusement is actually an adaptation of the Elizabethan game, hoodman blind.*

# A Time of Contrasts

As with almost everything else about the Elizabethan era, the ways people amused themselves were highly contrasted. It seems difficult to conceive of the idea, for instance, that the same people who enjoyed watching one of William Shakespeare's dramas one day would be in a front row seat at a bearbaiting the next, or that the man who was smacking an opponent in cudgel play also played the lute while waiting for the barber.

Such contrasts arose in other aspects of Elizabethan life, too. The time of Queen Elizabeth I was gaudy and almost grotesque in its clothing, in the amount of food served, and in the lavish decorations and displays in the prodigy houses. There was wealth and elegance, music and dance, yet those things were only paper thin. Behind them lurked coarseness, brutality, intolerance of the poor and sick, and the threat of an agonizing death from the plague.

It is to their credit, maintains historian William Stearns Davis, that the people of Elizabeth's London were able to strike a balance between the two extremes: "There is enormous joy in life and satisfaction in the mere act of living. If the

*The age of Elizabeth (pictured) was a time of stark contrast, but life in London balanced the extremes.*

realm and epoch produce their full share of wordlings and scoundrels, they produce more than their share of those choicer spirits who can spring only from a healthy people in a healthy age."[112]

# Notes

## Introduction: Elizabeth's London

1. Quoted in Alan Axelrod, *Elizabeth I, CEO: Strategic Lessons from the Leader Who Built an Empire.* Paramus, NJ: Prentice-Hall, 2000, p. 1.
2. Quoted in R.E. Pritchard, ed., *Shakespeare's England: Life in Elizabethan and Jacobean Times.* Gloucestershire, England: Sutton, 1999, p. 155.
3. Quoted in Michael Justin Davis, *The Landscape of William Shakespeare.* Devon, England: Webb & Bower, 1987, p. 129.
4. Quoted in Pritchard, *Shakespeare's England*, p. 198.
5. Quoted in Pritchard, *Shakespeare's England*, p. 156.

## Chapter 1: An Infinite Order

6. Jeffrey L. Singman, *Daily Life in Elizabethan England.* Westport, CT: Greenwood, 1995, p. 10.
7. Quoted in Singman, *Daily Life in Elizabethan England*, p. 12.
8. Elizabeth Burton, *The Pageant of Elizabethan England.* New York: Charles Scribner's Sons, 1958, p. 24.
9. Quoted in Dorothy Hartley and Margaret M. Elliot, *Life and Work of the People of England*, vol. 4. London: B.T. Batsford, 1925, p. 12.
10. Quoted in Burton, *The Pageant of Elizabethan England*, p. 42.
11. Quoted in Jo McMurtry, *Understanding Shakespeare's England: A Companion for the American Reader.* Hamden, CT: Archon Books, 1989, p. 17.
12. Quoted in McMurtry, *Understanding Shakespeare's England*, p. 17.
13. M. St. Clare Byrne, *Elizabethan Life in Town and Country.* New York: Barnes and Noble, 1961, p. 112.
14. Quoted in Pritchard, "*Shakespeare's England*, p. 206.
15. Quoted in Byrne, *Elizabethan Life in Town and Country*, p. 113.
16. Quoted in Byrne, *Elizabethan Life in Town and Country*, p. 114.
17. Quoted in Singman, *Daily Life in Elizabethan England*, p. 18.
18. Quoted in Allardyce Nicoll, *The Elizabethans.* Cambridge, England: Cambridge University Press, 1957, p. 99.

## Chapter 2: Marriage and Family

19. Quoted in "Elizabethan England: A Compendium of Common

Knowledge, 1558–1603." www.renaissance.dm.net.

20. Quoted in Thomas Rogers Forbes, *Chronicle from Aldgate: Life and Death in Shakespeare's London.* London: Yale University Press, 1971, p. 37.

21. Quoted in Forbes, *Chronicle from Aldgate*, pp. 29–30.

22. Quoted in McMurtry, *Understanding Shakespeare's England*, p. 121.

23. Quoted in Pritchard, *Shakespeare's England*, p. 46.

24. Quoted in Byrne, *Elizabethan Life in Town and Country*, p. 196.

25. Quoted in Nicoll, *The Elizabethans*, p. 100.

26. Quoted in Byrne, *Elizabethan Life in Town and Country*, p. 206.

27. Quoted in Nicoll, *The Elizabethans*, p. 107.

## Chapter 3: A London Home

28. Quoted in Byrne, *Elizabethan Life in Town and Country*, p. 48.

29. Quoted in L.F. Salzman, *England in Tudor Times: An Account of Its Social Life and Industries.* London: B.T. Batsford, 1933, p. 75.

30. Quoted in Burton, *The Pageant of Elizabethan England*, p. 47.

31. Quoted in Burton, *The Pageant of Elizabethan England*, p. 67.

32. Quoted in Nicoll, *The Elizabethans*, p. 91.

33. Quoted in A.F. Scott, *The Tudor Age.* New York: Thomas Y. Crowell, 1975, p. 33.

34. Quoted in Scott, *The Tudor Age*, p. 34.

35. Quoted in Scott, *The Tudor Age*, p. 20.

36. Quoted in Pritchard, *Shakespeare's England*, p. 156.

37. Davis, *The Landscape of William Shakespeare*, p. 35.

38. Quoted in Elizabeth Burton, *The Pageant of Stuart England.* New York: Charles Scribner's Sons, 1962, p. 168.

## Chapter 4: Elizabethan Fashion

39. Quoted in Pritchard, *Shakespeare's England*, p. 131.

40. Quoted in editors of Time-Life Books, *What Life Was Like: In the Realm of Elizabeth, England,* AD *1533–1603.* Alexandria, VA: Time-Life, 1998, p. 154.

41. Quoted in Scott, *The Tudor Age*, p. 74.

42. Quoted in editors of Time-Life Books, *All the Rage.* Alexandria, VA: Time-Life, 1992, p. 77.

43. Phyllis G. Tortora and Keith Eubank, *Survey of Historic Costume: A History of Western Dress.* New York: Fairchild, 1994, p. 160.

44. Quoted in editors of Time-Life Books, *All the Rage*, p. 79.

45. Quoted in Byrne, *Elizabethan Life in Town and Country*, p. 67.

46. Quoted in editors of Time-Life Books, *What Life Was Like*, p. 154.

47. Quoted in Scott, *The Tudor Age*, pp. 76, 78.

48. Quoted in Drea Leed, "Elizabethan Make-Up 101," *Elizabethan Costuming Page*. www.dnaco.net.
49. Quoted in Burton, *The Pageant of Elizabethan England*, p. 237.
50. Quoted in Leed, "Elizabethan Make-Up 101."
51. Quoted in editors of Time-Life Books, *All the Rage*, p. 42.
52. Editors of Time-Life Books, *All the Rage*, p. 42.

## Chapter 5: At the Table

53. Quoted in Scott, *The Tudor Age*, p. 45.
54. Quoted in Burton, *The Pageant of Elizabethan England*, p. 140.
55. Quoted in Alison Sim, *Food and Feast in Tudor England*. New York: St. Martin's, 1997, p. 45.
56. Quoted in William Stearns Davis, *Life in Elizabethan Days: A Picture of a Typical English Community at the End of the Sixteenth Century*. New York: Harper & Row, 1930, p. 81.
57. Quoted in Davis, *The Landscape of William Shakespeare*, p. 155.
58. Quoted in Sim, *Food and Feast*, pp. 148–49.
59. Quoted in Burton, *The Pageant of Elizabethan England*, p. 145.
60. Quoted in Philippa Pullar, *Consuming Passions: Being an Historic Inquiry into Certain English Appetites*. Boston: Little, Brown, 1970, p. 124.
61. Quoted in Burton, *The Pageant of Elizabethan England*, p. 146.
62. Pullar, *Consuming Passions*, pp. 98–99.
63. Quoted in Sim, *Food and Feast*, p. 143.
64. Quoted in Pullar, *Consuming Passions*, p. 86.
65. Quoted in "Folger Shakespearean Library, Fooles and Fricassees: Food in Shakespeare's England," September 10–December 30, 1999. www.folger.edu.
66. Quoted in Sim, *Food and Feast*, p. 105.
67. Quoted in Sim, *Food and Feast*, p. 110.

## Chapter 6: "Lord, Have Mercy upon London"

68. Quoted in F.P. Wilson, *The Plague in Shakespeare's London*. London: Oxford University Press, 1963, p. 25.
69. Quoted in Wilson, *The Plague in Shakespeare's London*, p. 30.
70. Quoted in Wilson, *The Plague in Shakespeare's London*, p. 29.
71. Quoted in Wilson, *The Plague in Shakespeare's London*, p. 34.
72. Quoted in Penry Williams, *Life in Tudor England*, New York: G.P. Putnam's Sons, 1964, p. 104.
73. Quoted in Byrne, *Elizabethan Life in Town and Country*, p. 55.
74. Quoted in Byrne, *Elizabethan Life in Town and Country*, p. 283.
75. Quoted in Scott, *The Tudor Age*, p. 122.
76. Quoted in Byrne, *Elizabethan Life in Town and Country*, p. 283.
77. Jasper Ridley, *The Tudor Age*. Woodstock, NY: Overlook, 1988, p. 252.
78. Davis, *Life in Elizabethan Days*, p. 165.

79. Quoted in Ridley, *The Tudor Age*, p. 249.
80. Wilson, *The Plague in Shakespeare's London*, p. 2.
81. Quoted in Nicoll, *The Elizabethans*, p. 66.
82. Quoted in Pritchard, *Shakespeare's England*, p. 176.
83. Quoted in Wilson, *The Plague in Shakespeare's London*, p. 44.
84. Quoted in Wilson, *The Plague in Shakespeare's London*, p. 59.
85. Quoted in Pritchard, *Shakespeare's England*, p. 176.

## Chapter 7: Crime in Elizabethan London

86. Quoted in Salzman, *England in Tudor Times*, p. 60.
87. Quoted in Scott, *The Tudor Age*, pp. 182–83.
88. Quoted in Salzman, *England in Tudor Times*, p. 59.
89. Quoted in Scott, *The Tudor Age*, p. 196.
90. Salzman, *England in Tudor Times*, pp. 60–61.
91. Quoted in Salzman, *England in Tudor Times*, p. 64.
92. McMurtry, *Understanding Shakespeare's England*, p. 165.
93. Quoted in William Andrews, *Old-Time Punishments*. London: Simpkin, Marshall, Hamilton, Kent, 1890, p. 202.
94. Andrews, *Old-Time Punishments*, p. 126.
95. Andrews, *Old-Time Punishments*, p. 39.

96. Andrews, *Old-Time Punishments*, p. 42.
97. Quoted in Levi Fox, *Shakespeare's England*. New York: G.P. Putnam's Sons, 1972, p. 58.
98. Quoted in Fox, *Shakespeare's England*, p. 58.
99. Quoted in McMurtry, *Understanding Shakespeare's England*, p. 157.
100. Quoted in Scott, *The Tudor Age*, pp. 168–69.
101. McMurtry, *Understanding Shakespeare's England*, p. 161.

## Chapter 8: Pleasure and Sport

102. Quoted in Singman, *Daily Life*, p. 149.
103. Quoted in Byrne, *Elizabethan Life in Town and Country*, p. 255.
104. Davis, *Life in Elizabethan Days*, p. 240.
105. Quoted in Singman, *Daily Life*, p. 153.
106. Quoted in Davis, *The Landscape of William Shakespeare*, p. 135.
107. Quoted in Byrne, *Elizabethan Life in Town and Country*, p. 299.
108. Burton, *The Pageant of Elizabethan England*, p. 188.
109. Quoted in Byrne, *Elizabethan Life in Town and Country*, p. 241.
110. Quoted in Byrne, *Elizabethan Life in Town and Country*, p. 241.
111. Quoted in Davis, *The Landscape of William Shakespeare*, p. 80.
112. Davis, *Life in Elizabethan Days*, p. 6.

# For Further Reading

## Books

Jane Ashelford, *A Visual History of Costume: The Sixteenth Century*. London: Batsford, 1983. Ashelford offers good information with invaluable illustrations showing Elizabethan dress, especially in paintings of the era.

Phillis Cunnington and Catherine Lucas, *Occupational Costume in England: From the Eleventh Century to 1914.* London: Adam and Charles Black, 1976. Excellent quotations and drawings fill this book, which also contains a very complete bibliography.

Herbert Norris, *Tudor Costume and Fashion*. Mineola, NY: Dover, 1997. Norris provides an excellent section on hairstyles for men and women.

Jasper Ridley, *The Tudor Age*. Woodstock, NY: Overlook, 1988. This book includes a very complete bibliography and index; it also contains good information on Elizabethan fashion.

Marion Sichel, *History of Men's Costume*. London: Batsford Academic and Educational, 1984. This work offers helpful information and has a particularly detailed glossary.

# Works Consulted

William Andrews, *Old-Time Punishments*. London: Simpkin, Marshall, Hamilton, Kent, 1890. Andrews offers vivid detail of scold's bridle and the death penalty.

Leonard Ashley, *Elizabethan Popular Culture*. Bowling Green, OH: Bowling Green State University Popular Press, 1988. An excellent source for primary quotations and information on songs and family life.

Alan Axelrod, *Elizabeth I, CEO: Strategic Lessons from the Leader Who Built an Empire*. Paramus, NJ: Prentice-Hall, 2000. This book offers good information on the background of Elizabeth as well as the obstacles she faced during her reign.

Elizabeth Burton, *The Pageant of Elizabethan England*. New York: Charles Scribner's Sons, 1958. A very readable account, with good information on the furnishings of houses of the age.

———, *The Pageant of Stuart England*. New York: Charles Scribner's Sons, 1962. Though dealing with a period after Elizabethan England, the author includes some information that applies to both eras and a good index.

M. St. Clare Byrne, *Elizabethan Life in Town and Country*. New York: Barnes and Noble, 1961. This work contains an excellent chapter on childhood and education; it also includes a very helpful index and bibliography.

Michael Justin Davis, *The Landscape of William Shakespeare*. Devon, England: Webb & Bower, 1987. This source provides helpful quotations, with good material on sports and activities.

William Stearns Davis, *Life in Elizabethan Days: A Picture of a Typical English Community at the End of the Sixteenth Century*. New York: Harper & Row, 1930. This book has good information on the legal system and criminals of the era.

Editors of Time-Life Books, *All the Rage*. Alexandria, VA: Time-Life, 1992. A highly entertaining volume with superb illustrations; it also contains a very good section on codpieces.

———, *What Life Was Like: In the Realm of Elizabeth, England, AD 1533–1603*. Alexandria, VA: Time-Life, 1998. This work contains excellent photographs and illustrations as well as good sidebar material about social history.

Thomas Rogers Forbes, *Chronicle from Aldgate: Life and Death in Shakespeare's London*. London: Yale

University Press, 1971. This book features interesting primary quotations, which are especially helpful when learning about the toll the plague took on London.

Levi Fox, *Shakespeare's England*. New York: G.P. Putnam's Sons, 1972. Although limited text, this book contains excellent illustrations of various aspects of Elizabethan life.

Elizabeth Lane Furdell, *The Royal Doctors, 1485–1714: Medical Personnel at the Tudor and Stuart Courts*. Rochester, NY: University of Rochester Press, 2001. Although difficult to read, this book provides invaluable information on the medical knowledge of the era, especially about the plague.

Dorothy Hartley and Margaret M. Elliot, *Life and Work of the People of England* Vol. 4. London: B. T. Batsford, 1925. Though a very old work, it is both terse and well organized, with very interesting illustrations.

Jo McMurtry, *Understanding Shakespeare's England: A Companion for the American Reader*. Hamden, CT: Archon Books, 1989. This extremely well-written and American-friendly book provides explanations for historical questions. It also contains excellent sections on city life and social rank.

Allardyce Nicoll, *The Elizabethans*. Cambridge, England: Cambridge University Press, 1957. An excellent collection of primary quotations with very complete notes.

R.E. Pritchard, ed., *Shakespeare's England: Life in Elizabethan and Jacobean Times*. Gloucestershire, England: Sutton, 1999. A very rich collection of quotations from writers and historians of the era.

Philippa Pullar, *Consuming Passions: Being an Historic Inquiry into Certain English Appetites*. Boston: Little, Brown, 1970. Pullar provides good information on the Elizabethan kitchen plus an appendix that provides a number of recipes of the era.

L.F. Salzman, *England in Tudor Times: An Account of Its Social Life and Industries*. London: B.T. Batsford, 1933. Salzman provides a good section on the homes and furnishings of Elizabethan homes.

A.F. Scott, *The Tudor Age*. New York: Thomas Y. Crowell, 1975. This book provides an excellent bibliography and selection of primary quotations as well as helpful thumbnail biographies of quotation sources.

Alison Sim, *Food and Feast in Tudor England*. New York: St. Martin's, 1997. A very readable book with good details on every aspect of meals and food; also contains excellent endnotes.

Jeffrey L. Singman, *Daily Life in Elizabethan England*. Westport, CT: Greenwood, 1995. This book contains excellent illustrations and diagrams as well as detailed information on costumes and fashion of the era.

Pamela H. Smith and Paula Findlen, eds., *Merchants and Marvels: Commerce, Science, and Art in Early Modern Europe.* London: Routledge, 2002. This work offers excellent information with thoroughly documented notes as well as a helpful index and illustrations.

Phyllis G. Tortora and Keith Eubank, *Survey of Historic Costume: A History of Western Dress.* New York: Fairchild, 1994. A very complete book offering a good bibliography and colorful illustrations.

Penry Williams, *Life in Tudor England.* New York: G.P. Putnam's Sons, 1964. Sections on the plague in England and sections of Elizabethan homes and furnishings are very helpful.

F.P. Wilson, *The Plague in Shakespeare's London.* London: Oxford University Press, 1963. An excellent source for information on sanitary conditions in London; includes a helpful index and complete footnotes.

**Internet Sources**

"Elizabethan England: A Compendium of Common Knowledge, 1558–1603." www.renaissance. dm.net. Although the site does not include much information on aspects of the common person's life in Elizabethan England, some good information is provided, such as background on marriage and family.

Folger Shakespearean Library, "Fooles and Fricassees: Food in Shakespeare's England," September 10–December 30, 1999. www.folger.edu. This online article offers helpful information with lots of detail.

Drea Leed, "Elizabethan Make-Up 101," *Elizabethan Costuming Page.* www.dnaco.net. An excellent website with a wide range of period commentary on makeup and hairstyles.

# Index

torture, 79–81
Tower of London, 79–80
trade, 43
trade associations. *See* guilds
tradesmen, 17
traveling, 77
*Tudor Age, The* (Scott), 32, 73, 82, 91

universities, 32

Vaughan, William, 28

water, 38, 40, 66
weddings, 25–26
Williams, Penry, 68
*Winter's Tale, The* (Shakespeare), 51
witchcraft, 83–85

Wolsey, Thomas, 15
women
  childbearing and, 27
  clothing of, 43–46, 47
  cosmetics and, 50–52, 53
  crimes of, 82, 83–85
  education of, 29, 30, 31
  marriage and, 23, 24
  rights of, 21–22
  work of, 40, 41–42
Woolley, Hannah, 63
workers, 19–20
  *see also* guilds
worldview, 12–13
wrestling, 92

yeomen, 17, 19

# Picture Credits

# About the Author

Gail B. Stewart received her undergraduate degree from Gustavus Adolphus College in St. Peter, Minnesota. She did her graduate work in English, linguistics, and curriculum study at the University of St. Thomas and the University of Minnesota. She taught English and reading for more than ten years.

She has written over ninety books for young people, including a series for Lucent Books called The Other America. She has written many books on historical topics such as World War I and the Warsaw ghetto.

Stewart and her husband live in Minneapolis with their three sons, Ted, Elliot, and Flynn; two dogs; and a cat. When she is not writing, she enjoys reading, walking, and watching her sons play soccer.